# SBAC
# TEST PREP

# GRADE 3

# CALIFORNIA

# ENGLISH
## LANGUAGE ARTS

Origins Publications

We help students develop their higher-order thinking skills while also improving their chances of admission into gifted and accelerated-learner programs.

Our goal is to unleash and nurture the genius in every student. We do this by offering educational and test prep materials that are fun, challenging and provide a sense of accomplishment.

Please contact us with any questions.

info@originspublications.com

Copyright © 2018 by Origins Publications

Written and Edited by: California Test Prep Team

**ISBN: 13: 978-1-948255-45-5**

Origins Publications
New York, NY, USA
Email:info@originspublications.com

# TABLE OF CONTENTS

Introduction ............................................................................................ 4

How To Use This Book ........................................................................... 5

Test Prep Tips ........................................................................................ 6


**Reading: Literature** ............................................................................ 7

Ask & Answer Questions Using Text Evidence (3.RL.1.1) ....................... 8

Recount Stories & Determine Theme (3.RL.1.2) ................................... 13

Describe Characters & Explain Their Actions (3.RL.1.3) ....................... 17

Determine Word Meaning In Context (3.RL.2.4) ................................... 21

Identify & Understand Parts Of Texts (3.RL.2.5) .................................. 23

Identify Point Of View of Self & Author/Characters (3.RL.2.6) ............. 26

Identify How Illustrations Convey Information (3.RL.3.7) ...................... 29

Compare & Contrast Narratives (3.RL.3.9) .......................................... 32


**Reading: Information** ......................................................................... 36

Ask & Answer Questions Using Text Evidence (3.RI.1.1) ....................... 37

Determine Main Idea & Explain Key Details (3.RI.1.2) .......................... 41

Describe & Understand Relationships Between Ideas (3.RI.1.3) ............. 45

Determine Domain-Specific Word Meaning in Context (3.RI.2.4) ........... 49

Use Text Features & Search Tools (3.RI.2.5) ......................................... 53

Identify Point Of View of Self & Author (3.RI.2.6) ................................. 56

Use & Understand Information In Illustrations (3.RI.3.7) ....................... 60

Describe & Make Connections In Text (3.RI.3.8) ................................... 63

Compare And Contrast Key Points In Two Texts (3.RI.3.9) .................... 67


**Language** ............................................................................................ 70

Demonstrate Command of Grammar & Usage (3 .L.1.1) ........................ 71

Know Capitalization, Punctuation & Spelling (3.L.1.2) ........................... 73

Use Appropriate Language Conventions (3.L.2.3) .................................. 75

Determine Meaning of Unknown Word/s in Context (3.L.3.4) ................ 78

Understand Word Relationships and Nuances in Meaning (3.L.3.5) ........ 80

Know Academic/Domain-Specific Words (3.L.3.6) ................................. 82


**Answer Key and Explanations** ............................................................ 85


**Practice Tests** .................................................................................... 97

Practice Test One .................................................................................. 99

Practice Test One Answer Key & Explanations ...................................... 123

Access to Bonus Practice Test Two ....................................................... 130

# INTRODUCTION

### The SBAC Assessments

The SBAC (Smarter Balanced Assessment Consortium) assessments are important tests designed to assess whether students are meeting the rigorous Common Core State Standards that have been implemented in schools across America. These standards, or learning goals, outline what students in each grade should learn each year. These standards emphasize just how important the new goals are: they can help show whether students are on the right track to college and beyond, even when the students are years from those life stages.

SBAC is a consortium of US states which cooperate to develop and improve the Smarter Balanced Assessments.

### SBAC English Language Arts (ELA) Test

The SBAC ELA summative assessments are annual year-end tests that measure reading, writing, speaking, listening, and language skills. Like the Common Core Standards, SBAC assessments focus on higher level critical thinking skills, problem solving, analysis, and real-world application.

The ELA test includes the following topics:

**Reading**: Reading skills are measured by having students read a variety of literary and informational texts. Tasks sometimes require students to compare, analyze, or integrate information from multiple texts.

**Writing**: To demonstrate writing ability, students must compose, revise, and/or edit both shorter and longer literary and informational texts for a variety of purposes (narrative, informational/explanatory, and opinion/argumentative).

**Speaking and Listening:** For speaking and listening questions, students will listen to a variety of one-minute informational texts and respond to listening comprehension questions. The listening comprehension questions are very similar in content to the reading comprehension questions.

**Research and Inquiry:** The research and inquiry questions focus on the ability to paraphrase text, identify credible sources, and evaluate the strength of information to support a claim or for a stated purpose.

The ELA assessment consists of two parts: a Computer Adaptive Test (CAT) and a Performance Task (PT). The CAT administers the same amount of questions to each student, but customizes each student's assessment. Questions become easier when a student answers incorrectly and more difficult when a student answers correctly.

In Grades 3-5, the PT prompts students to gather, select and analyse information in a series of sources, including two short texts. Students also write a narrative that demonstrates grade-appropriate writing and research skills.

### Question Format on SBAC ELA Assessments

In addition to the Performance Task, students taking the SBAC ELA assessment may be asked to respond to several types of questions. These include:

**Selected response questions**. These can require a single answer, where students select the correct response from four answer choices, or multiple answers, where a student must select a specified number of answers that s/he thinks best responds to the question.

**Constructed response.** A student is expected to produce answers in one or two complete sentences within the space, usually an answer box.

**Non-traditional response** (or technology enhanced) items include questions that may ask students to drag and drop text, edit text, complete a chart or graphic organizer, etc.

# HOW TO USE THIS BOOK

The objective of this book is to provide students, educators, and parents with practice materials focused on the core skills needed to help students succeed on the SBAC assessment.

A student will fare better on an assessment when s/he has practiced and mastered the skills measured by the test. A student also excels when s/he is familiar with the format and structure of the test. This book helps students do both. Students can review key material by standard through doing the skill-building exercises, as well as take practice tests to become accustomed to how the content is presented and to enhance test-taking skills. By test day, students will feel confident and be adequately prepared to do his or her best.

## This Book Includes:

- 196 skill-building exercises organised by standard in order to help students learn and review concepts in the order that they will likely be presented in the classroom. These worksheets also help identify weaknesses, and highlight and strengthen the skills needed to excel on the actual exam. A variety of question types are included in the worksheets to help students build skills in answering questions in multiple formats, so they don't get tripped up by perplexing or unfamiliar question types on test day.

- Practice test materials that are based on the official SBAC assessments released by the test administrator, and include similar question types and the same rigorous content found on the official assessments. By using these materials, students will become familiar with the types of items (including Technology Enhanced questions, presented in a paper based format) they may see on the real test.

- Answer keys with detailed explanations to help students not make the same mistakes again. These explanations help clear up common misconceptions and indicate how students might arrive at an answer to a question.

- Answer keys also identify the standard/s that the question is assessing. If a student is having difficulty in one area, encourage the student to improve in that area by practicing the specific set of skills in the workbook.

- Test prep tips to help students approach the test strategically and with confidence.

# TEST PREP TIPS

First of all, remind your student to pay attention in class throughout the year, asking questions as needed on homework and classwork. The Language Arts curriculum should follow the exact standards and skills that will be tested on the end-of-year assessment.

One of the best ways to prepare for a reading test is by—of course—reading. In the months leading up to the test, have your student read a certain amount of pages or minutes weekly from a book that she enjoys. Reading consistently will improve your student's reading comprehension and enhance her vocabulary, two skills that are crucial to success on the exam.

Another extremely effective strategy is to practice, practice, practice. Have your student work on practice questions and complete at several full length practice tests. Our practice tests are a great place to start.

However, simply answering the questions and then moving on will not yield much improvement. If your student misses a question, discuss why the correct answer is indeed correct. Come up with alternate approaches to this question type that may work better in the future. Have your student explain her answer to each question. This gives you the opportunity to reinforce logical thinking and correct misconceptions as needed. Plus, it's good practice for finding evidence to support a claim, perhaps the key skill on ELA reading assessments.

Prior to the test, encourage students to get a solid night of sleep and eat a nourishing breakfast.

For children, avoiding test anxiety is very important, so be sure to avoid over-emphasizing the test or inadvertently causing your student to feel excessive stress or pressure.

In addition, **teach your student general test-taking strategies such as the following:**

Narrow down your answer choices by using process of elimination. This involves crossing out obviously wrong answers to increase your chances of finding the correct answer.

If you get stuck on a question, skip it and come back to it after answering easier questions.

Remember that no one is expected to answer every single correction correctly. Don't panic when you get stuck on a question. Take a deep breath and remember that you are intelligent and prepared.

If you follow the tips here, your student should be well on her way to a stress-free and successful performance on this important assessment.

# READING: LITERATURE

# ASK & ANSWER QUESTIONS USING TEXT EVIDENCE

**RL.1.1: Ask and answer questions to demonstrate understanding of a text, referring explicitly to the text as the basis for the answers.**

*Directions: Read the passage and answer the questions that follow.*

## Passage 1: The Cheeses That Ran Away
### by Clifton Johnson

1    There was a man of Gotham who filled a sack with cheeses and started off for Nottingham market to sell them. He carried the sack on his back, and when he became tired he sat down by the wayside to rest. Thus he went on until he reached the summit of the last hill he had to climb before he came to Nottingham bridge.

2    There he rested, and when he rose to continue his journey a cheese slipped out of the sack and rolled down the hill toward the bridge.

3    "Ah! Mr. Cheese," said the man, "so you can run to market alone, can you? I wish I had known that before. It would have saved me the trouble of carrying you. Well, then, if you can go to market alone, so can the other cheeses, and I will send them along after you."

4    So he laid down his sack, took out the cheeses, and one by one rolled them down the hill. As the last one spun down the road he shouted, "I charge you all to meet me at the market-place."

5    Some of the cheeses went into one bush, and some went into another bush, but the man did not notice that, and he trudged on cheerfully to the market expecting the cheeses would meet him there. All day long he loitered about the market, and as evening approached he began to inquire among his friends and neighbors and other men if they had seen his cheeses come to the market.

6    "Who should bring them?" asked one of the market-men.

7    "Nobody," replied the man of Gotham. "They would bring themselves. They know the way well enough."

1. This question has two parts. First, answer Part A. Then, answer Part B.
## Part A
Where does the man believe his cheeses are going?
> **A.** He thinks they're going into the bushes.
> **B.** He thinks they're running away.
> **C.** He thinks they're meeting him at the marketplace.
> **D.** He thinks they're going back home.

## Part B

Which piece of evidence from the passage best supports your answer to Part A?

**A.** "Well, then, if you can go to market alone, so can the other cheeses, and I will send them along after you." (Paragraph 3)

**B.** "So he laid down the sack, took out his cheeses, and one by one rolled them down the hill." (Paragraph 4)

**C.** "There was a man of Gotham who filled a sack with cheeses and started off for Nottingham market to sell them." (Paragraph 1)

**D.** "Then he rested, and when he rose to continue his journey a cheese slipped out of the sack and rolled down the hill toward the bridge." (Paragraph 2)

2. What is one piece of evidence from the story that gives you a clue that the cheeses will likely not find their way to market?

**A.** "As the last one spun down the road he shouted, 'I charge you all to meet me at the market-place.'"

**B.** "Some of the cheeses went into one bush, and some went into another bush, but the man did not notice that…"

**C.** "Then he rested, and when he rose to continue his journey a cheese slipped out of the sack and rolled down the hill toward the bridge."

**D.** ""Ah! Mr. Cheese," said the man, "so you can run to market alone, can you? I wish I had known that before."

3. What detail from the text tells why the man rolled his cheeses down the hill after the first cheese escaped?

_____

_____

_____

4. What do you think will happen next in the story?

**A.** The cheeses will come to the marketplace and the man will sell them.

**B.** The man will never find his cheeses.

**C.** The man will find out that one of the other villagers took his cheeses.

**D.** The cheeses will come to the marketplace too late.

## Passage 2: The Kettle That Would Not Walk
**by Clifton Johnson**

1    One day a Gotham man was getting ready to go to market, and his wife said to him, "Husband, we need a new iron kettle for the fireplace. Don't fail to buy one."

2    So the man bought a kettle at Nottingham, and toward evening he took it on his arm and started for home. But the kettle was heavy, and at length his arm grew tired with carrying it and he set it down. While he was resting he noticed that the kettle had three legs. "What a pity I did not see those legs before!" cried the man. "Here you have three legs and I have but two, and yet I have been carrying you. 'Twere fairer that you had carried me. Well, you shall take me the rest of the way, at least."

3    Then he seated himself in the kettle and said, "Now, go on; I am all ready;" but the kettle stood stock still on its three legs and would not move.

4    "Ah!" said the man, "you are stubborn, are you? You want me to keep on carrying you, I suppose; but I shall not. I will tell you the way and you can stay where you are until you get ready to follow me."

5    So he told the kettle where he lived and how to get there, and then off the man went. When he reached home his wife asked him where the kettle was.

6    "Oh, it will be along in good time," he replied.

7    "And what do you mean by that?" said she.

8    "Why," said he, "the kettle I bought has three legs, and was better able to walk here from Nottingham market than I who have but two legs. Yet I never noticed it had legs until I was nearly here. Then I told it to walk the rest of the way itself, for I would carry it no farther."

9    "Where did you leave it?" asked the wife.

10   "You need not be anxious," responded the man.

11   "I told it the way, and it will be along in good time, as I said before."

12   "And where did you leave it?" again asked the wife.

13   "At Gotham bridge," he replied.

14   She was not so sure about its coming as he was and she hurried off to get it, and when she brought it home the man said, "I am glad you have it safe, wife, for I have been thinking while you were gone that it might have taken a notion to walk back to Nottingham if we had left it alone there in the road much longer."

5. The man and his wife have different opinions about leaving the kettle to walk home on its own. Describe the man's opinion and the wife's opinion. Use details from the passage to support your answer.

Man's Opinon:

_____

_____

_____

Supporting Detail:

_____

_____

_____

Wife's Opinon:

_____

_____

_____

Supporting Detail:

_____

_____

_____

6. Which detail from the text explains why the man believes the kettle should carry him instead?

_____

_____

_____

_____

7. In what way are the cheeses from Passage 1 and the kettle from Passage 2 similar?
   A. They both refuse to walk.
   B. They both disobey their owners.
   C. They both run away.
   D. They both are sold in a marketplace in the end.

8. This question has two parts. First, answer Part A. Then, answer Part B.

## Part A

What sentence describes the woman's feelings at the end of the passage?

    **A.** She agrees with the man that the kettle will come home eventually.

    **B.** She thinks the kettle will walk back to Nottingham.

    **C.** She doesn't think the kettle will come home.

    **D.** She thinks the man is lying and never really bought a kettle.

## Part B

What happens as a result of the woman's feelings in Part A?

    **A.** The woman gets mad at the man.

    **B.** The woman goes to get the kettle and bring it home.

    **C.** The woman tells the man to go get the kettle.

    **D.** The woman and the man wait for the kettle to arrive.

# RECOUNT STORIES & DETERMINE THEME

**RL.1.2. Recount stories, including fables, folktales, and myths from diverse cultures; determine the central message, lesson, or moral and explain how it is conveyed through key details in the text.**

*Directions: Read the passage and answer the questions that follow.*

## Passage 1: The Ant and the Grasshopper
### Adapted from the fable by Aesop

1    In a field one summer's day a Grasshopper was hopping about, chirping and singing to its heart's content.  An Ant passed by, carrying an ear of corn he was taking to the nest.

2    "Why not come and chat with me," said the Grasshopper, "instead of working in that way?"

3    "I am helping to lay up food for the winter," said the Ant," and recommend you do the same."

4    "Why bother about winter?" said the Grasshopper. "We have got plenty of food at present."  But the Ant went on its way and continued its work.

5    A few days later, the Grasshopper was playing a game with his friends when the Ant passed by, again bearing food.

6    "Take a break and come play with us," the Grasshopper urged the Ant.

7    "Winter is coming soon," the Ant told him. "I have to ensure my family has enough food."

8    "We have many days left until winter," said the Grasshopper. "All that work isn't necessary." But the Ant ignored the Grasshopper and continued its work.

9    When the winter came, the Grasshopper had no food and found itself dying of hunger. Every day, he saw the ants distributing the corn and grain they had collected in the summer.

1.  Using the details from "The Ant and the Grasshopper," complete the sequence of events below.

(1) The Grasshopper asks the Ant to chat with him, but the Ant says he is putting away food for the winter.

(2) _____

(3) The Grasshopper again sees the Ant and asks him to come play with him, but the Ant says he has to make sure his family has enough food for winter.

(4) The Grasshopper says there is plenty of time left until winter and the Ant's work isn't necessary.

(5) _____

2. What is a main lesson in the fable "The Ant and the Grasshopper?"

_____

_____

_____

_____

3. Which detail helps to convey the fable's lesson?

**A.** "An Ant passed by, bearing along carrying an ear of corn he was taking to the nest."

**B.** "'Winter is coming soon,' the Ant told him."

**C.** "In a field one summer's day a Grasshopper was hopping about, chirping and singing to its heart's content."

**D.** "When the winter came, the Grasshopper had no food and found itself dying of hunger."

4.  Why doesn't the Grasshopper want to work like the Ant? Use information from the passage to support your answer.

_____

_____

_____

_____

_____

_____

## Passage 2: The Story of Icarus
### Adapted from Greek mythology

1   A very long time ago on the island of Crete, a father and his son Icarus were imprisoned in a cave high above the sea. They had been imprisoned because the father was an extremely talented inventor, and the greedy King wanted the father to work only for him.

2   As Icarus became a teenager, he began to want a life of his own outside of the cave.

3   Icarus' father asked the King if he could let Icarus go, but the King refused his request.

4   When the father saw the disappointed face of his son Icarus, he knew that he must find a way for Icarus to escape. He gazed out of the cave and noticed seagulls flying high over the waves. At that moment, he had an idea.

5   For many days, the father and son collected seagull feathers. The father used metal frames to create two pairs of man-sized wings, and he attached the seagull feathers with candle wax.

6   On the day they planned to leave, the father reminded his son, "Icarus, remember not to fly too close to the sun. If you do, the wax will melt and you'll lose your feathers. Just follow my path." Icarus agreed.

7   As the father and son started to fly, Icarus loved the freedom he felt. He watched the seagulls soar higher and higher and decided to follow them.

8   "Icarus, stop!" yelled his father. "If you fly too high, the wax will melt. Not so high, Icarus!"

9   But Icarus didn't listen. As he flew even higher, he started to feel the wax melting down his arms. He saw his feathers slipping off and falling into the ocean. Icarus tried to fly lower, but it was too late.

10   The father watched in horror as his son fell into the water. He flew to shore to try to save his son, but he found nothing except a few seagull feathers floating in the ocean.


5. What is a lesson that readers can learn from the myth "The Story of Icarus?"

_____

_____

_____

_____

6. Which detail from the passage helps to convey the lesson in this myth?

   **A.** "As Icarus became a teenager, he began to want a life of his own outside of the cave."

   **B.** "As the father and son started to fly, Icarus loved the freedom he felt."

   **C.** "But Icarus didn't listen. As he flew even higher, he began to feel the wax melting down his arms."

   **D.** "For many days, the father and son collected seagull feathers."

7. Why are the father and Icarus imprisoned?

   **A.** They committed a crime.

   **B.** The King wanted Icarus' father to make inventions only for him.

   **C.** Icarus is dangerous.

   **D.** The King is evil and dislikes Icarus' father.

8. What would be another good title for this myth?

   **A.** The Greedy King

   **B.** Flying

   **C.** The Inventor and His Inventions

   **D.** The Disobedient Son

# DESCRIBE CHARACTERS & EXPLAIN THEIR ACTIONS

**RL.1.3 Describe characters in a story (e.g., their traits, motivations, or feelings) and explain how their actions contribute to the sequence of events.**

*Directions: Read the passage and answer the questions that follow.*

## Passage 1: The Camping Trip

1   All week long, Jessica and her friend Tia had been planning their first camping trip. It wasn't technically a real camping trip, since it would be in Tia's backyard, but they were determined to make it as close to camping in the woods as possible.

2   The girls planned to make smores, tell ghost stories, and look at the stars.

3   The day of the camp out finally arrived, and it was all Jessica and Tia could talk about at school. Later that night, the girls set up their sleeping bags in Tia's backyard. They made a pretend tent by throwing a sheet over some tree branches.

4   First, the girls decided to make smores. "You brought the marshmallows, right Jessica?" asked Tia.

5   "Oh no!" said Jessica. "I forgot the marshmallows!"

6   Tia didn't want to make Jessica feel bad, so she said, "That's okay. We can just eat chocolate and graham crackers!" It wasn't the same, but the girls pretended they were eating real smores.

7   Next, they decided to look at the stars. But the sky was dark and overcast, and there were no stars to be seen.

8   "Well, let's try telling ghost stories," said Tia. The girls started telling spooky stories, and they were having a great time. Then, suddenly, big drops of rain started pouring down.

9   The girls ran inside. Instead of feeling disappointed, they started planning an even better camping trip for another day.

1.  Many problems happen on Tia and Jessica's camp out. What do Tia and Jessica's reactions to these problems tell you about them?
    **A.** They don't like camping very much.
    **B.** They both have positive attitudes.
    **C.** They will probably never try to camp again.
    **D.** They have a good sense of humor.

2. When Jessica forgets the marshmallows, Tia says, "That's okay. We can just eat chocolate and graham crackers!" What does this tell you about Tia as a character?

    **A.** She's a good friend.

    **B.** She doesn't like marshmallows.

    **C.** She's selfish.

    **D.** She's forgetful.

3. Would you like to be friends with Jessica and Tia? Use details from the story to support your answer.

    _____

    _____

    _____

    _____

    _____

    _____

4. Select two details that show Tia and Jessica are flexible when things don't go the way they planned.

    ☐ "The girls planned to make smores, tell ghost stories, and look at the stars." (Paragraph 2)

    ☐ "It wasn't the same, but the girls pretended they were eating real smores." (Paragraph 6)

    ☐ "The girls started telling spooky stories, and they were having a great time." (Paragraph 8)

    ☐ "Instead of feeling disappointed, they started planning an even better camping trip for another day." (Paragraph 9)

## Passage 2: Leaf Games

1   Lauren pouted as she dragged the rake across the fallen leaves for what felt like the hundredth time. "I'm going to be out here all day," she sighed.

2   Just then, her neighbor Drew rode by on his red bicycle. "Hey!" said Drew. "You look like you could use some help."

3   Lauren was shocked. She couldn't imagine that anyone would ever volunteer to help with such a boring task. "Are you sure?" she asked.

4   Drew got off his bike and walked over to Lauren. "Of course!" he said. "Let's do a leaf jump." Drew ran and jumped into one of the piles Lauren had raked, scattering leaves everywhere.

5   "You try!" said Drew.

6   Lauren ran and jumped into another pile. "That is pretty fun!" she said, laughing. "But we're making a big mess."

7   Drew looked around. "True," he said. "Okay, let's do a race. You use this rake and I'll use this one. We have to race across the yard while dragging the rake behind us to rake these leaves. First one to the other side wins. Got it?"

8   "Got it!" said Lauren. She and Drew started running across the yard, dragging the rakes behind them. Drew got to the other side first, but Lauren challenged him to a rematch. "It was my first try!" she explained.

9   At dinner that night, Lauren's parents told her she had done a great job raking the leaves. "That might have to be your chore from now on," said Lauren's dad.

10  Lauren smiled. "Okay!" she said. "Raking leaves isn't so bad."

5.  How does Lauren's attitude about raking leaves change from the beginning of the story to the end? Use details from the passage to support your answer.

_____

_____

_____

_____

_____

6. This question has two parts. First, answer Part A. Then, answer Part B.

## Part A

How is Drew in Passage 2 similar to Jessica and Tia in Passage 1?

    **A.** He can make the best of a bad situation.

    **B.** He likes the outdoors.

    **C.** He has a good sense of humor.

    **D.** He's good at playing games.

## Part B

What detail from Passage 2 best supports your answer in Part A?

    **A.** "Just then, her neighbor Drew rode by on his red bicycle." (Paragraph 2)

    **B.** "Drew got off his bike and walked over to Lauren." (Paragraph 4)

    **C.** "'Of course!' he said. 'Let's do a leaf jump!'" (Paragraph 4)

    **D.** "'You try!' said Drew." (Paragraph 5)

7. Do you think that Drew is a good friend? Use details from the passage to support your response.

_____

_____

_____

8. How do Lauren and Drew's feelings about raking leaves at the beginning of the passage differ? Use details from the passage to support your answer.

Lauren:

_____

Supporting Detail:

_____

_____

Drew:

_____

Supporting Detail:

_____

_____

# DETERMINE WORD MEANING IN CONTEXT

**RL.2.4 Determine the meaning of words and phrases as they are used in a text, distinguishing literal from nonliteral language.**

*Directions: Answer the questions below.*

It was the day of the school spelling bee, and I was sitting on the stage waiting for my turn. My palms were sweating, and **my heart was beating like a drum.** I had practiced for weeks, but I worried that I would suddenly forget all of the words I had studied.

1. Determine the meaning of the bolded phrase above.
   **A.** The author is very excited.
   **B.** The author is feeling sick.
   **C.** The author isn't prepared for the spelling bee.
   **D.** The author is nervous.

2. Josie was so sleepy and bored that she **dozed off** right there on the couch.
   What is the meaning of the bolded phrase above?

   _____

   _____

3. Benny was very careful as he walked across the old bridge. He knew that if he made one wrong move, he would **plunge** straight down into the water below.
   What detail(s) in the text above helps the reader know the meaning of the word **plunge?**

   _____

   _____

4. We all have challenges in life. We all have our mountains to climb. For me, it's math class. Math isn't easy for me. But I know if I work hard and keep trying, I'll make it to the top one day.
   What does the author compare his struggles in math class to?

   _____

   _____

5. Liz was so **swift** that she won every race at school, and it was never even close.
   What does the word **swift** mean in the above sentence?
   - **A.** Fast
   - **B.** Athletic
   - **C.** Clever
   - **D.** Brave

6. After we kicked the soccer ball into Old Man Frank's yard, almost everyone was too scared to go and get it. But not Peter. He walked right into the mean man's yard. Peter had **nerves of steel.**
   What does the phrase **nerves of steel** mean in the sentence above?
   - **A.** Determination
   - **B.** Patience
   - **C.** Courage
   - **D.** Kindness

7. Peter walked into the backyard, and we couldn't see him anymore. We anxiously looked at one another, worried about what would happen next. We all **caught our breath** and listened for the sound of Old Man Frank yelling. At first, we didn't hear anything.
   What detail in the text above helps the reader know what the phrase **caught our breath** means?
   - **A.** "Peter walked into the backyard…"
   - **B.** "…and listened for the sound of Old Man Frank yelling."
   - **C.** "…and we couldn't see him anymore."
   - **D.** "…worried about what would happen next."

8. But soon, we heard it: Old Man Frank. Except he wasn't yelling. He was just talking to Peter, asking him questions like, "How often do you boys play soccer?" He even told Peter a story about when he played soccer as a young boy. Maybe all of our **assumptions** about Old Man Frank had been wrong. It seemed like he wasn't so scary after all.
   What are two details in the text above that help you to understand the meaning of the word **assumptions**?

   _____

   _____

   _____

   _____

   _____

# IDENTIFY & UNDERSTAND PARTS OF TEXTS

**RL.2.5 Refer to parts of stories, dramas, and poems when writing or speaking about a text, using terms such as chapter, scene, and stanza; describe how each successive part builds on earlier sections.**

*Directions: Answer the questions below.*

1. A paragraph is to a story like a stanza is to _____.
   **A.** A topic
   **B.** A poem
   **C.** An illustration
   **D.** Words

2. A paragraph is to a story like a _____ is to a play.
   **A.** Stanza
   **B.** Scene
   **C.** Character
   **D.** Text Feature

3. What is the main purpose of line breaks in a poem?
   **A.** To organize the poem into chapters.
   **B.** To help the reader read with emotion.
   **C.** To enhance ideas and meaning.
   **D.** To let the reader take a breath.

4. When does the author usually introduce the characters and describe the setting in a story? Explain why.

   _____

   _____

   _____

   _____

5. When is a story's problem usually solved? Explain why.

   _____

   _____

   _____

## The Sheep
**Ann and Jane Taylor**

*Directions: Read the poem and answer the questions that follow.*

1　"Lazy sheep, pray tell me why
　　In the pleasant fields you lie,
　　Eating grass, and daisies white,
　　From the morning till the night?
　　Everything can something do,
　　But what kind of use are you?"

2　"Nay, my little master, nay,
　　Do not serve me so, I pray;
　　Don't you see the wool that grows
　　On my back, to make you clothes?
　　Cold, and very cold, you'd be
　　If you had not wool from me.

3　True, it seems a pleasant thing,
　　To nip the daisies in the spring;
　　But many chilly nights I pass
　　On the cold and dewy grass,
　　Or pick a scanty dinner, where
　　All the common's brown and bare.

4　Then the farmer comes at last,
　　When the merry spring is past,
　　And cuts my woolly coat away,
　　To warm you in the winter's day:
　　Little master, this is why
　　In the pleasant fields I lie."

6. How many stanzas does this poem have?
　　**A.** 5
　　**B.** 4
　　**C.** 10
　　**D.** 16

7.  Which lines describe best why the master should appreciate the sheep?

    **A.** True, it seems a pleasant thing,
    To nip the daisies in the spring;

    **B.** But many chilly nights I pass
    On the cold and dewy grass,

    **C.** Don't you see the wool that grows
    On my back, to make you clothes?

    **D.** Everything can something do,
    But what kind of use are you?"

8.  Read these lines from the poem:

    Then the farmer comes at last,
    When the merry spring is past,
    And cuts my woolly coat away,
    To warm you in the winter's day:

    Why do you think the author included this information?

    **A.** To help readers imagine how a woolly coat can keep them warm.
    **B.** To show that the main benefit of owning a sheep comes in winter, not spring.
    **C.** To show that winter will soon arrive.
    **D.** To suggest that the farmer would like a woolly coat.

# IDENTIFY POINT OF VIEW OF SELF & AUTHOR/CHARACTERS

**RL.2.6 Student should be able to distinguish own point of view from that of the narrator or those of the characters.**

---

*Directions: Answer the questions below.*

1. What is a story's point of view?
   **A.** How the characters are introduced.
   **B.** The story's lesson or moral.
   **C.** Who is narrating or telling the story.
   **D.** The problem that must be solved in the story.

2. What is a third-person point of view?
   **A.** When a character in the story is the narrator and uses words like I, me, and we.
   **B.** When the narrator is not part of the story and uses words like he, she, and they.
   **C.** When there is only one character in the story.
   **D.** When the main character is the first person mentioned in the story.

*Directions: Read the passage below and answer the questions.*

## Home at Last

1   It was cold and rainy outside, but I had nowhere to go. I hid under some bushes to try to shield myself from the rain.

2   Later, I tried to run across the street to find better shelter. Drivers honked angrily as their cars almost hit me. "Get out of the way!" someone yelled.

3   The rain was slowing down, but now I was hungry. I walked around looking for food. Someone threw a bread crust on the sidewalk, so I ran over to eat it. "Get lost!" a man yelled as I walked across his path.

4   But then another man saw me and bent down, smiling. "Hi, little puppy," he said. "Aren't you cute?"

5   It was the first time someone had been nice to me in days. I wagged my tail happily.

6   "Are you lost?" he asked. "Do you have anywhere to go?"

7   I wanted to explain to the man that I didn't have a home, but he seemed to understand anyway. "Do you want to come home with me?" he asked.

8   I wagged my tail again. The man picked me up, put me in his car, and drove me to his house.

9  "A dog?" asked his wife. "Are you crazy? We don't need a dog."

10  I was scared that I would have to go back outside, but the man asked his wife, "Please, Susie?" The woman agreed, but she didn't look very happy.

3. This question has two parts. First, answer Part A. Then, answer Part B.

**Part A**
Who is the narrator of this story?
> **A.** A man
> **B.** A woman
> **C.** A puppy
> **D.** A young boy

**Part B**
What character in the story gives the reader insight as to the narrator's identity?
> **A.** The man who yells, "Get out of the way!"
> **B.** The man who brings the puppy home.
> **C.** The woman
> **D.** The rain

4.  From what point of view is this story written?
> **A.** First person
> **B.** Second person
> **C.** Third person
> **D.** Fourth person

5.  What does the author do to make you feel bad for the puppy? Use details from the passage to support your answer.

_____

_____

_____

_____

_____

6. What is the feeling of the narrator at the beginning of this story?
> **A.** Happy
> **B.** Bored
> **C.** Cold
> **D.** Tired

7. This question has two parts. First, answer Part A. Then, answer Part B.

**Part A**

What detail in the story best shows the woman's point of view about the dog?

    **A.** "The woman agreed..."

    **B.** "...but she didn't look very happy."

    **C.** "I was scared that I would have to go back outside."

    **D.** "The man asked his wife, 'Please, Susie?'"

**Part B**

What information about the dog might change the woman's point of view?

    **A.** The dog is homeless.

    **B.** The dog needs a bath.

    **C.** The dog has fleas.

    **D.** The dog is scared of humans.

8. How do the other human characters in the story have a different point of view than the man who takes the dog home? Use details from the story to support your response.

 

 

 

 

 

 

 

 

# IDENTIFY HOW ILLUSTRATIONS CONVEY INFORMATION

**RL.3.7 Explain how specific aspects of a text's illustrations contribute to what is conveyed by the words in a story (e.g., create mood, emphasize aspects of a character or setting).**

*Directions: Read the text and observe the images below, then answer the questions.*

## Passage 1: The First Day of School

Nathan and Julie were twins and best friends. They never got to be in the same class, but third grade was different. This year, Nathan and Julie had the same teacher!

The twins had just gotten home from the first day of third grade, and all they could talk about was how nice their new teacher seemed. Most of their best friends were also in the same class.

Some of the topics they would be learning about seemed a little challenging, but Nathan and Julie were confident that third grade would be a good year.

1.  What do you think is happening in this picture? Why?

_____

_____

_____

_____

2.  How do the characters (Nathan and Julie) feel in this picture? Why do you think so? Use evidence from both the text and the pictures to support your response.

_____

_____

_____

_____

3. What clues does the author give you to show you that Nathan and Julie are confident that third grade will be a great year? Use at least one piece of evidence from both the text and the pictures to support your response.

_____

_____

_____

## Passage 2: My Giant Dog

I have the friendliest, sweetest dog in the world. He's also enormous. My dog is so big that a lot of people think he's scary or mean.

But his heart is just as big as the rest of him. Whenever I'm feeling sad, he notices and comes to cuddle with me. He walks my little brother and me to the school bus every morning to make sure we're safe. When we get home from school, he greets us enthusiastically, wagging his tail and trying to lick us. I can't imagine a better dog. My older sister even taught him to dance!

From my giant dog, I've learned not to judge others based on their appearance. My dog may be a giant, but he's not mean or scary.

4. What physical characteristic about the dog does this image emphasize?
   - **A.** The dog is hungry
   - **B.** The dog is enormous.
   - **C.** The dog is cute.
   - **D.** The dog is funny.

5. What character trait of the dog's does this image emphasize?
   - **A.** He's mean.
   - **B.** He's scary and intimidating.
   - **C.** He's scared.
   - **D.** He's sweet and loving.

6. What is the purpose of the image above? How does it add to the information in the text?

_____

_____

_____

7. Look at the image below.

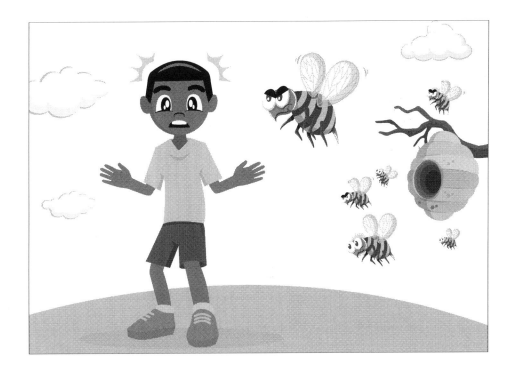

How do you think the boy is feeling in the picture above? Explain why.

_____

_____

_____

_____

_____

_____

# COMPARE & CONTRAST NARRATIVES

**RL.3.9 Compare and contrast the themes, settings, and plots of stories written by the same author about the same or similar characters (e.g., in books from a series).**

*Directions: Read the passages below and answer the questions.*

## Passage 1: The Goose and the Golden Egg
**Adapted from the fable by Aesop**

1   There was once a farmer who owned a golden goose. Every day, the goose laid a beautiful, shiny golden egg.

2   People came from far and wide to see the magnificent goose and her golden eggs. The farmer began taking the eggs to market, and people would pay large amounts of money to buy them.

3   The farmer was getting richer than he had ever imagined. But he wanted more. The goose only gave the farmer one egg each day, and the farmer decided this was not enough. He became impatient with the goose.

4   One day, the farmer was counting his money when an idea came to him. If he cut the goose open, he could get all of the golden eggs at once. That way, he wouldn't have to wait for one egg each day, and he could make much more money.

5   Imagining what he would do with his riches, the farmer cut the goose. To his disappointment, he didn't find even one golden egg inside. His plan had failed!

6   And now the farmer's precious golden goose was dead. He would never lay another golden egg.

## Passage 2: The Dog and His Reflection
**Adapted from the fable by Aesop**

1   One day, a dog was running past the butcher's shop. The butcher threw the dog a bone. The excited dog began hurrying home with his delicious prize.

2   As the dog was crossing a bridge, he looked down and saw his reflection in the water. But the dog didn't realize that he was looking at his reflection. Instead, he

thought he was looking at another dog. And he thought the other dog had a much bigger bone in his mouth!

3   If the dog had stopped to think for a minute, he might have realized his mistake. But instead of thinking, he dropped his bone and jumped at the dog in the river. He was hoping to take the bigger bone for himself.

4   Instead of getting a bone, the dog found himself having to swim frantically to shore. He finally reached the shore and dragged himself out of the water.

5   Now instead of having a bigger bone, the dog had no bone at all. He stood on the shore, thinking sadly about the delicious bone he had lost.

1.  How are the farmer and the dog alike in these two stories? Use details from the passages to support your response.

_____

_____

_____

_____

_____

_____

_____

2. This question has two parts. First, answer Part A. Then, answer Part B.
**Part A**
What is the setting of the first passage?
   **A.** A river
   **B.** A farm
   **C.** A mountain
   **D.** A school

**Part B**
What is the setting of the second passage?
   **A.** A river
   **B.** A farm
   **C.** A mountain
   **D.** A school

3. This question has two parts. First, answer Part A. Then, answer Part B.

## Part A

Which of the following could be a theme of both stories?

    **A.** Make good choices.

    **B.** Be careful who you trust.

    **C.** Treat others the way that you want to be treated.

    **D.** Be grateful for what you have instead of being greedy.

## Part B

What detail from the first passage helps develop this theme?

    **A.** "People came from far and wide to see the magnificent goose and her golden eggs." (Paragraph 2)

    **B.** "The farmer was getting richer than he had ever imagined." (Paragraph 3)

    *C.* "The farmer was counting his money when an idea came to him." (Paragraph 4)

    **D.** "And now the farmer's precious golden goose was dead. He would never lay another golden egg." (Paragraph 6)

4.   What decision do the characters make in Passage 1 and in Passage 2, and what are the results?

The farmer's decision:

_____

_____

The result:

_____

_____

_____

The dog's decision:

_____

_____

The result:

_____

_____

_____

5. What is the problem in both stories?

    **A.** The main characters want more than what they have.

    **B.** Other characters try to take what the main characters have.

    **C.** The main characters both get lost.

    **D.** The main characters don't have enough money to buy something important.

6. What caused the farmer to cut open his goose? Use details from the story to support your answer.

_____

_____

_____

_____

7. Why did the dog jump into the river? Use details from the story to support your answer.

_____

_____

_____

_____

8. Select the sentences below that show how the farmer and the dog are different

    ☐ The farmer wants more money, while the dog wants a bigger bone.

    ☐ The farmer mistakenly thinks he can get more eggs if he cuts open the goose, while the dog mistakenly thinks his reflection is another dog with a bigger bone.

    ☐ The dog loses his bone and the farmer accidentally kills his goose.

    ☐ A farmer gave the dog a bone, while the farmer gets his golden goose from the market

    ☐ The dog's story takes place on a river, while the farmer's story takes place on a farm.

    ☐ The farmer is happy at the end of the story, while the dog is scared at the end of the story.

# READING: INFORMATION

# ASK & ANSWER QUESTIONS USING TEXT EVIDENCE

**RI.1.1 Ask and answer questions to demonstrate understanding of a text, referring explicitly to the text as the basis for the answers.**

*Directions: Read the passage and answer the questions that follow.*

## Passage 1: About the Starfish

1  Marine scientists are trying to change the name "starfish" to "sea star" because the name isn't accurate. Why? The starfish is not a fish.

2  Like fish, the starfish does live underwater. However, it doesn't have scales, gills, or fins. It can only live in saltwater. The starfish is actually an echinoderm, like sand dollars and sea urchins.

3  Around the world, there are about 2,000 different species of starfish. Most of them have five arms, but some have 10 arms, 20 arms, or even 40 arms. They have hard, bony skin that can protect them from predators. Most of them also have bright colors that can scare off predators or be used as camouflage to hide from predators.

4  Starfish, or sea stars, are very unique animals. They have one eye on the tip of each arm, and their eyes can't see color. They don't have brains or blood. Instead of blood, starfish have sea water running through their bodies.

5  If a starfish loses an arm, they have the amazing ability to make it grow back. Some species can even grow a whole new sea star from a broken arm.


1.  The name "starfish" is not accurate because the starfish
    **A.** does not look like a star.
    **B.** is not a fish.
    **C.** doesn't live underwater.
    **D.** has scales, but not fins or gills.


2.  Which of the following is NOT a way that starfish protect themselves from predators?
    **A.** Their skin is hard and bony.
    **B.** They use their bright colors to scare predators.
    **C.** They have sharp spikes on each arm.
    **D.** They also use their bright colors as camouflage to hide from predators.

3. List three things that make the starfish a unique animal.

    1. _____

    2. _____

    3. _____

4. How many arms does the starfish have? Use evidence from the text to support your answer.

    _____

    _____

    _____

    _____

    _____

    _____

## Passage 2: The Starfish Killer

1   Back in 2012, millions of starfish started dying out across North America. A mysterious starfish killer turned these sea stars into piles of "white goo" or "white slime."

2   Recently, scientists have discovered exactly what has been killing starfish. It's a type of parvovirus. The virus causes starfish to become weak, and it leaves them open to bacterial infections. The bacterial infection kills the sea star.

3   About 8-17 days after infection, the starfish starts to develop white sores on its body. Sometimes, the starfish's arms rip off and walk away. Eventually, the starfish melts into a pile of white goo.

4   This virus isn't new, but scientists aren't sure what's causing it to kill so many starfish. In the past, the virus only attacked one or two species at a time. Now,over 20 species of starfish have been affected, including the sunflower star, the giant pink star, and the rainbow star.

5   Some scientists think the virus is spreading so quickly because there are so many sea stars packed into small areas.

6   Scientists are continuing to study this parvovirus to see if they can stop it. If they can't stop it, scientists hope to be able to prevent it from happening again in the future.


5.  Using details from the passage, complete the sequence of events below.

   (1) The starfish catches the parvovirus.

   (2) _____

   (3) The starfish gets a bacterial infection.

   (4) _____

   (5) _____

   (6) The starfish melts into a pile of white goo.

6.  Where is the parvovirus mostly killing starfish?
   **A.** North America
   **B.** Around the world
   **C.** Asia
   **D.** The Caribbean

7. The following question has two parts. First, answer Part A. Then, answer Part B.

## Part A

The parvovirus isn't new. But what is different about the virus nowadays?

     **A.** It's affecting starfish all over the world.

     **B.** It's affecting many different species of starfish.

     **C.** It's turning starfish to white goo.

     **D.** It's killing starfish in days instead of weeks.

## Part B

What do scientists think the reason is for the change in Part A?

     **A.** The virus is growing more powerful.

     **B.** Starfish aren't as strong as they were in the past.

     **C.** There are large numbers of starfish packed into small areas.

     **D.** This is a different type of parvovirus.

8. Based on the details in the passage, what inference can be made about how scientists will respond to the parvovirus? Use details from the passage to support your answer.

_____

_____

_____

_____

_____

_____

_____

# DETERMINE MAIN IDEA & EXPLAIN KEY DETAILS

**RI.1.2 Determine the main idea of a text; recount the key details and explain how they support the main idea.**

*Directions: Read the passage and answer the questions that follow.*

## Passage 1: The Invention of the Potato Chip

1    Have you ever eaten a potato chip and wondered how this salty treat was invented? Maybe through lots of time, effort, and experimenting?

2    Actually, the answer might surprise you. The potato chip was invented completely by accident. A hotel chef named George Crum cooked some fried potatoes for his customers. But the customers thought George's fried potatoes were disgusting. They complained that the potatoes were too thick and too bland, or flavorless.

3    George Crum was furious that the customers had complained about his food. He decided to teach them a lesson. George grabbed some more potatoes and sliced them until they were as thin as a piece of paper. Next, he put an excessive amount of salt on them.

4    George was sure that the customers would think that these fried potatoes were even worse, and they would learn to appreciate his delicious food.

5    Instead, the customers loved the new fried potatoes! Soon, everyone was talking about the tasty potato chips that George Crum had invented.

6    So next time you eat a bag of potato chips, remember that it all started with a hotel chef trying to prank his rude customers.

1. Select the statement that describes the main idea of the article.
   **A.** George Crum was not a very nice chef.
   **B.** Potato chips were invented by accident.
   **C.** Customers should be polite, not rude.
   **D.** Sometimes our plans don't go the way we expect.

2. List at least two details that support the main idea.

........................................................................................

........................................................................................

........................................................................................

........................................................................................

3. Which quote from the passage best supports the main idea?

    **A.** "George Crum was furious that the customers had complained about his food." (Paragraph 3)

    **B.** "They complained that the potatoes were too thick and too bland, or flavorless." (Paragraph 2)

    **C.** "So next time you eat a bag of potato chips, remember that it all started with a hotel chef trying to prank his customers." (Paragraph 6)

    **D.** "Instead, the customers loved the new fried potatoes!" (Paragraph 5)

4. What is another title that could be used for this passage?

    **A.** The Rude Customers

    **B.** The Angry Chef

    **C.** Hotel Cooking Adventures

    **D.** Potato Chips: A Happy Accident

## Passage 2: The Invention of Baseball

1    Until 2011, popular legend was that a man named Abner Doubleday invented the sport of baseball. Abner Doubleday was a man who eventually fired one of the first shots in the Civil War, and he became a heroic general.

2    According to the legend, 20-year-old Doubleday invented the sport in 1939 in Cooperstown, New York. He used a stick to draw his idea for baseball in the dirt. It was a new game he had invented that he and his friends could play.

3    The story was so popular that the National Baseball Hall of Fame was opened in Cooperstown, New York, where baseball was supposedly invented.

4    But the truth is that Doubleday did not invent baseball. Major League Baseball's historian, John Thorn, published a book explaining that baseball was played long before 1939. As early as the 1800's, different versions of baseball were played in New York, Philadelphia, and Massachusetts. A similar bat and ball game, called Rounders, was also played in Britain.

5    So who did invent baseball? Historian John Thorn says that this is one question that will probably never be answered.

5. Which of the following best describes the main idea of this passage?
   **A.** Despite the popular legend that Abner Doubleday invented baseball, we don't know who actually invented the sport.
   **B.** Different versions of baseball were played in New York, Philadelphia, Massachusetts, and even Britain.
   **C.** According to legend, 20-year-old Abner Doubleday invented the sport of baseball in Cooperstown, New York in 1939.
   **D.** John Thorn published a book explaining that Abner Doubleday did not invent baseball, because baseball was being played long before 1939.

6. List at least two details that support or develop the main idea.

_____

_____

_____

_____

_____

7. Which of the following quotes does NOT support the main idea of this passage?

　　**A.** "As early as the 1800's, different versions of baseball were played in New York, Philadelphia, and Massachusetts." (Paragraph 4)

　　**B.** "The story was so popular that the National Baseball Hall of Fame was opened in Cooperstown, New York, where baseball was supposedly invented." (Paragraph 3)

　　**C.** "But the truth is that Doubleday did not invent baseball." (Paragraph 4)

　　**D.** "Abner Doubleday was a man who eventually fired one of the first shots in the Civil War, and he became a heroic general." (Paragraph 1)

8. Who invented baseball?

　　**A.** Abner Doubleday

　　**B.** John Thorn

　　**C.** We'll probably never know.

　　**D.** Someone in Britain who called the game "Rounders."

# DESCRIBE & UNDERSTAND RELATIONSHIPS BETWEEN IDEAS

**RI.3.3 Describe the relationship between a series of historical events, scientific ideas or concepts, or steps in technical procedures in a text, using language that pertains to time, sequence, and cause/effect.**

*Directions: Read the passage and answer the questions that follow.*

## Passage 1: The Sinking of The Titanic

1    On April 15, 1912, a huge steamship called the Titanic hit an iceberg and sank to the bottom of the Atlantic Ocean. Over 1,500 people drowned in the tragic accident. It was the very first time the Titanic had sailed.

2    At the time, the Titanic was the largest ship that had ever been built. It had a swimming pool, a gym, several cafes, a library, a barber shop, and more. People believed it was "the safest ship ever."

3    Because people thought the ship was unsinkable, there were only 20 lifeboats on board. This was enough to hold only half of the passengers and crew. Nothing bad could happen to the Titanic, people thought. But when something bad did happen, there weren't enough lifeboats to get everyone to safety.

4    The Titanic also received at least five warnings that there was ice ahead, but the warnings were ignored. Some historians say that the captain, Edward J. Smith, was trying to cross the Atlantic faster than another ship, the Olympic. For an icy area, the Titanic was traveling way too fast.

5    If the ship had been moving slower, they might have seen the iceberg in time. The ship also might have hit the iceberg with less force and caused less damage.

1. Why were there only 20 lifeboats on board the Titanic?
    **A.** 20 was the correct number of lifeboats for a ship that size.
    **B.** People thought that the Titanic was unsinkable.
    **C.** It was too expensive to buy more lifeboats.
    **D.** 20 lifeboats would hold all of the passengers and crew.

2. Why do many historians believes the Titanic was traveling so fast?
    **A.** The captain wanted to beat the speed of another ship.
    **B.** They were trying to get away from the icebergs.
    **C.** There was a storm coming, and the captain wanted to beat it.
    **D.** The Titanic was traveling the appropriate speed.

3. What are two factors that made the Titanic accident worse? Use evidence from the text to support your response.

_____

_____

_____

_____

_____

_____

4. How did people's beliefs about the Titanic affect what happened to the ship? Use details from the text to support your answer.

_____

_____

_____

_____

_____

_____

## Passage 2: The Great Chicago Fire

1    In 1871, almost the entire city of Chicago was made of wood. There were wooden buildings, wooden sidewalks, and even wooden streets. Therefore, it's no surprise that the Great Chicago Fire of October 8, 1871 spread quickly and caused major damage.

2    The week before the Great Chicago Fire, there were 20 fires in the city. The firefighters were exhausted when they got a call on October 8th around 9:00 PM that a fire had started behind the O'Leary home. Catherine and Patrick O'Leary lived in the home with their five children.

3    At first, the firefighters were sent to the wrong neighborhood. By the time they finally got to the O'Leary house, the fire was out of control. The fire continued to burn for two days until rain fell and extinguished it. Thousands of buildings burnt down, and hundreds of people died in the fire.

4    Mrs. O'Leary explained to reporters that she was sleeping when the fire started. But newspapers reported that she was milking her cow in the barn and the cow kicked over a lantern, starting the terrible fire. Almost everyone in Chicago blamed Mrs. O'Leary for the destructive fire. After the fire, everyone was so angry with Mrs. O'Leary that she stayed in her house and avoided other people.

5    Architects rebuilt Chicago with the world's first skyscrapers. The population and the economy grew, and Chicago became a great city again.


5.  List at least two reasons that the Great Chicago Fire spread so quickly.

_____

_____

_____

_____

_____

_____


6.  Why was the fire out of control by the time the firefighters got to the O'Leary house?
    **A.** Mrs. O'Leary was sleeping when the fire started.
    **B.** Mrs. O'Leary's cow had kicked over the lantern.
    **C.** The firefighters were sent to the wrong neighborhood first.
    **D.** The firefighters were sleeping and took too long to get to the house.

7. Who or what did the people of Chicago blame for the fire?

    **A.** The wooden buildings, sidewalks, and streets

    **B.** Mrs. O'Leary and her cow

    **C.** The exhausted firefighters who went to the wrong neighborhood

    **D.** Mrs. O'Leary's five children

8. What was one positive effect of the Chicago Fire? Use details from the passage to support your response.

_____

_____

_____

_____

9. How did the Chicago Fire change Mrs. O'Leary's life? Use details from the passage to support your answer.

_____

_____

_____

_____

10. What finally stopped The Great Chicago Fire?

    **A.** The Chicago firefighters

    **B.** The rain

    **C.** A team of volunteers

    **D.** Firefighters from neighboring cities

11. How are Passage 1 (The Sinking of the Titanic) and Passage 2 (The Great Chicago Fire) similar? Be sure to use at least 1 detail from each passage to support your answer.

_____

_____

_____

_____

_____

_____

_____

# DETERMINE DOMAIN-SPECIFIC WORD MEANING IN CONTEXT

**RI.2.4 Determine the meaning of general academic and domain-specific words and phrases in a text relevant to a grade 3 topic or subject area.**

*Directions: Read the passage and answer the questions that follow.*

## Passage 1: The Cactus Plant

1    The cactus is a type of plant known as a succulent. It can store water to drink later if it doesn't rain for a long time. Cacti (more than one cactus plant) can store water in their stems, roots, and leaves. In fact, a cactus plant can live for an entire year without rain.

2    How does the cactus plant store so much water? Its spikes, which are actually called spines, help prevent the water from escaping. The cactus plant's waxy skin helps it hold in water too.

3    When you envision a cactus plant, you probably picture a spiky green plant. Actually, there are about 2,000 different types of cacti. Most are green, but some have a bluish or brownish hue. Some are flat and some are round, and they come in many unique shapes. They also grow large flowers that can be yellow, red, pink, white, orange, or blue. Some cacti even grow fruit.

4    Cacti do grow mostly in the desert or in other dry areas because they require dry, rocky soil. However, some cacti have been found in rainforests or as far north as Canada.

5    Cactus plants are most prevalent in Arizona, California, and Texas. People visit from all over just to see the many cacti that grow in these states, especially when the flowers are blooming between the months of March and May.

1.  What is the meaning of the underlined word as it is used in this sentence from the passage?

    Cactus plants are most <u>prevalent</u> in Arizona, California, and Texas. (Paragraph 5)
    - **A.** common
    - **B.** beautiful
    - **C.** large
    - **D.** opular

2. What is a succulent? Use details from the passage to support your answer.

_____

_____

_____

_____

_____

_____

3. What is the meaning of the underlined word as it is used in this sentence from the passage?

   Most are green, but some have a greenish or brownish <u>hue.</u> (Paragraph 3)
   - **A.** flower
   - **B.** color
   - **C.** fruit
   - **D.** skin

4. What is the meaning of the underlined word as it is used in this sentence from the passage?

   When you <u>envision</u> a cactus plant, you probably picture a spiky green plant. (Paragraph 3)
   - **A.** see
   - **B.** describe
   - **C.** draw
   - **D.** imagine

## Passage 2: The Cocoa Bean

1    If you've ever enjoyed a chocolate bar, chocolate cake, or chocolate ice cream, then you've eaten cocoa beans. Cocoa beans grow on trees in tropical climates, and they're used to make chocolate.

2    Cocoa trees only grow close to the Equator because they need hot and somewhat wet weather to flourish. The trees also need shade to grow, so they usually grow in the shade of other plants, such as mango and papaya trees.

3    Cocoa trees produce orange fruit, called pods. The pods have seeds on the inside, and these seeds are what we call cocoa beans. The beans are a milky white color at first, and they would taste extremely bitter if you ate them right off the tree.

4    To transform these bitter cocoa beans into delicious chocolate, chocolatiers have to first dry out the beans. Once the beans are dry, they become brownish-red in color.  They're then transported to a chocolate factory, where the beans are roasted.

5    The roasted cocoa beans are chopped into pieces called cocoa nibs. Heat and pressure are used to extract two liquids from the cocoa nibs: cocoa liquor and cocoa butter. These two liquids are mixed with sugar and milk powder, and we finally have the finished product!

6    The chocolate is sometimes poured into molds to give it a candy bar shape, then wrapped by a machine, and eventually placed on a shelf and purchased by kids like you. Who knew your favorite treat took such a journey to get to you?

5.  What is a chocolatier (Paragraph 4)? Use evidence from the text to support your answer.

_____

_____

_____

6.  What does the author mean by the underlined phrase in this sentence from the passage?

    These two liquids are mixed with sugar and milk powder, and we finally have the finished product! (Paragraph 5)
    A. Cocoa beans
    B. Cocoa nibs
    C. Chocolate
    D. Candy bars

7. What is the meaning of the underlined word as it used in this sentence from the passage?

   Heat and pressure are used to <u>extract</u> two liquids from the cocoa nibs: cocoa liquor and cocoa butter. (Paragraph 5)
   - **A.** make
   - **B.** remove
   - **C.** mix
   - **D.** carry

8. Select the **TWO** correct meanings of the word <u>journey</u> as it is used in the sentence.

   Who knew your favorite chocolate bar took such a <u>journey</u> to get to you? (Paragraph 6)
   - **A.** Traveling from one place to another
   - **B.** A fun trip or vacation
   - **C.** A long process
   - **D.** Hard work
   - **E.** Ocean voyage

# USE TEXT FEATURES & SEARCH TOOLS

**RI.2.5 Use text features and search tools (e.g., key words, sidebars, hyperlinks) to locate information relevant to a given topic efficiently.**

*Directions: Read the passage and answer the questions that follow.*

## Passage 1: Caves

1    A cave is a space under the surface of the Earth, in cliff walls, or in hillsides. Many times, caves are a complicated system of connected underground passageways, kind of like a maze.

### Types of Caves

2    Caves form over a long period of time, because the processes that make caves are very slow. There are several different processes that can make caves, and they form different types of caves.

3    **Solutional caves** are the most common, and they are formed from rainfall and chemical processes. The acid in the water eats away at the rock surface below, making a hole. The hole gets larger and larger, and eventually forms a cave.

4    Caves are also formed when hot lava from a volcano melts the rock surface below, making a hole.

5    **Sea caves** are formed when sea cliffs are eroded by waves and tides. The eroded cliff eventually forms a cave.

### Cave Features

6    Rock formations decorate most caves. These formations can hang down from the ceiling, sprout up from the ground, or cover the sides of a cave.

7    The most common formations are **stalactites** and **stalagmites**. Rock formations that hang from the ceiling are called stalactites. Rock formations that sprout up from the groundare called stalagmites. Both of these are formed from dripping water.

### Cave Creatures

8    Some animals like to spend time in cave entrances, but they don't live inside of caves. For example, foxes, bears, spiders, cockroaches, and frogs all like to take up shelter at cave entrances. Some birds may also build nests in cave entrances.

9    However, there are some animals that truly live in caves and these animals never go outside. Scientists who study caves, called **speleologists**, believe there are around 50,000 different species of animals that live in caves, and we will probably never discover them all.

1. What is the purpose of the headings in this passage?
   **A.** To tell the reader the author's opinion
   **B.** To help the reader visualize information
   **C.** To help the reader find the main idea of each section
   **D.** To help the reader place events in order

2. Why are some of the words in the paragraphs in bold text?
   **A.** To point out the main idea of the whole passage
   **B.** To draw the reader's attention to an important word
   **C.** To make the text look nice and easy to read
   **D.** To help the reader visualize information

3. What information can be found under the heading "Cave Features?"
   **A.** Caves are also formed when hot lava from a volcano melts the rock surface below.
   **B.** Some animals like to spend time in cave entrances but don't live in caves.
   **C.** Caves often hold a complicated system of connected underground passageways, kind of like a maze.
   **D.** Formations that hang from the ceiling are called stalactites.

4. Under which heading could the following information be added?

   "Technically, bats do not truly live in caves. This is because they sleep in caves, but they leave often to hunt for food."
   **A.** Cave Features
   **B.** Cave Creatures
   **C.** Types of Caves
   **D.** A new heading

5. Select the type text feature in the article that explains the difference between solutional caves and sea caves.
   **A.** Paragraphs
   **B.** Annotations
   **C.** Headings
   **D.** Subtitles

6. This question has two parts. First, answer Part A. Then, answer Part B.

## Part A

What is a sea cave?

    **A.** A cave formed from rainfall and chemical processes.

    **B.** A cave formed by an erupting volcano.

    **C.** A rock formation formed from dripping water.

    **D.** A cave formed when sea cliffs are eroded by waves and tides.

## Part B

Select the **TWO** text features you were able to use to find this information quickly.

    **A.** Footnote

    **B.** Headings

    **C.** Bold text

    **D.** Glossary

    **E**. Dictionary

7. If you wanted to search online for more information about the different types of caves, what words could you use to start your search?

    **A.** Solutional caves

    **B.** Cave features

    **C.** Animals that live in caves

    **D.** Cave Types

8. If the article included an alphabetical list of the bold words, along with their definitions, it would be called a/an:

    **A.** Glossary

    **B.** Index

    **C.** Hyperlink

    **D.** Caption

# IDENTIFY POINT OF VIEW OF SELF & AUTHOR

**RI.2.6 Distinguish their own point of view from that of the author of a text.**

*Directions: Read the passage and answer the questions that follow.*

## Passage 1: The Importance of Exercise

1    You probably know that exercise can make you strong and healthy, but being active might have more benefits than you realize.

2    Exercising regularly can help people maintain a healthy weight and prevent diseases like diabetes and high blood pressure. But it can also benefit your mind! Exercise produces endorphins, which are chemicals that help people feel happy and relaxed. And the more you exercise, the better your body and mind can handle situations that might make you feel stressed or anxious.

3    Exercising can also help people sleep better at night. Many people who exercise regularly feel more confident and energetic too.

4    Getting benefits from exercise doesn't require going to the gym every day or working out for hours. Just 30 minutes of physical activity can be extremely helpful. You can play a sport or a game with friends, go for a jog, ride a bike, dance, or even walk your dog. Just get up and move for 30 minutes a day, and you'll see wonderful benefits for your body and your mind.

1.   Select the **TWO** sentences from the passage that best help you understand the author's point of view.
   - ☐ "Just get up and move for 30 minutes a day, and you'll see wonderful benefits for your body and mind." (Paragraph 4)
   - ☐ "Exercising can help people sleep better at night." (Paragraph 3)
   - ☐ "You probably know that exercise can make you strong and healthy, but being active might have more benefits than you realize." (Paragraph 1)
   - ☐ "You can play a sport or a game with friends, go for a job, ride a bike, dance, or even walk your dog." (Paragraph 4)

2. This question has two parts. First, answer Part A. Then, answer Part B.

**Part A**

Based on the information in the passage, with which statement would the author most likely agree?

    **A.** Eating vegetables is also extremely important.

    **B.** Kids should spend more time outdoors.

    **C.** Exercise is important for physical and mental health.

    **D.** Everyone should go to the gym and exercise.

**Part B**

Which piece of evidence from the passage supports your answer in Part A?

    **A.** "Exercising regularly can help people maintain a healthy weight…" (Paragraph 2)

    **B.** "Getting benefits from exercise doesn't require going to the gym every day or working out for hours.

    **C.** "You can play a sport or game with your friends, go for a job, ride a bike, dance, or even walk your dog." (Paragraph 4)

    **D.** "Exercising regularly can help people maintain a healthy weight and prevent diseases like diabetes and high blood pressure. But it can also benefit your mind!" (Paragraph 2)

3. Based on the information in the passage, do you agree or disagree with the author's point of view? Why? What information in the passage influenced your point of view?

_____

_____

_____

_____

_____

_____

## Passage 2: Turn Off the TV

1    Kids today spend plenty of time looking at screens: computer screens, phone screens, and television screens. This isn't always a bad thing, but it should be done in moderation. Too much television, for example, can harm children.

2    Kids who consistently watch more than 4 hours of TV a day are more likely to be overweight and unhealthy. Kids who see violence on TV may be more aggressive. They may also start to believe that the world is a scary place and that something bad will happen to them.

3    Today's TV shows are also filled with bad behavior that can influence children to behave badly themselves. Commercials advertise unhealthy foods and drinks that can lead to an unhealthy lifestyle.

4    Plus, too much time spent watching TV can take time away from other, healthier activities. Kids who watch too much TV may spend less time playing outside, talking to friends and family, and reading or doing homework.

5    It's okay to watch an hour or two of TV a day, but don't overdo it. It can lead to an unhealthy lifestyle, bad behavior, and less time spent on more important activities. Do yourself a favor, and turn off the TV!

4. What is the author's point of view about television?
    **A.** It's okay to watch an hour or two of TV a day.
    **B.** Kids who see violence on TV may be more aggressive.
    **C.** Too much television can harm children.
    **D.** TV commercials advertise too many unhealthy foods and drinks.

5. What are the best words to show the author's point of view about television?
    **A.** Don't overdo it
    **B.** 4 hours of TV a day
    **C.** The world is a scary place
    **D.** Do yourself a favor

6. This question has two parts. First, answer Part A. Then, answer Part B.
## Part A
    Based on the information in the passage, with which statement would the author most likely agree?
    **A.** It's best for families to not own televisions.
    **B.** The television should be off during family dinner.
    **C.** Activities like reading and spending time with family are healthier than watching television.
    **D.** All kids who watch too much TV behave badly.

## Part B

What piece of evidence from the passage supports your answer in Part A?

**A.** "Kids who consistently watch more than 4 hours of TV a day are likelier to be overweight and unhealthy." (Paragraph 2)

**B.** "...too much time spent watching TV can take away from other, healthier activities. Kids who spend too much time watching TV may spend less time playing outside, talking to friends and family, and reading or doing homework." (Paragraph 4)

**C.** "They may also start to believe that the world is a scary place and that something bad will happen to them." (Paragraph 2)

**D.** "Today's TV shows are also filled with bad behavior that can influence children to behave badly themselves. Commercials advertise unhealthy foods and drinks that can lead to an unhealthy lifestyle." (Paragraph 3)

7. After reading the information in this passage, do you agree or disagree with the author's point of view? Be sure to use details from the passage to support your answer.

_____

_____

_____

_____

_____

8. How does the title of the article give you information about the author's point of view?

_____

_____

_____

_____

_____

# USE & UNDERSTAND INFORMATION IN ILLUSTRATIONS

**RI.3.7 Use information gained from illustrations (e.g., maps, photographs) and the words in a text to demonstrate understanding of the text (e.g., where, when, why, and how key events occur).**

*Directions: Read the passage and answer the questions that follow.*

## Passage 1: States of Matter

1    Matter is anything that takes up mass and space. In other words, matter is the "stuff" that the universe is made of. Matter is made up of atoms and molecules which combine to make up objects like the desk you're sitting in, the pencil you're holding, the paper you're reading, and even you. Matter exists in three main states (or forms): solids, liquids, and gases.

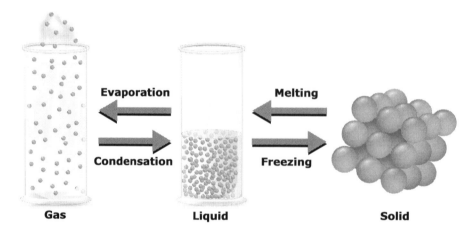

2    The air you're breathing right now is made of gases. Gas molecules are spread out and very energetic. They move around constantly. Gases are mostly invisible and have no fixed shape.

3    If you put a gas inside of a container, it will spread out to fill the whole container, no matter how big or small it is.

4    Liquids include water and soda. They are made up of molecules that aren't as spread out as gas molecules. But they're more spread out than solid molecules.

5    Liquid molecules can also move around easily, although they don't have as much energy as gas molecules. Liquids don't have their own shape. Instead, they take the shape of the container they're in.

6    Solids include you, your desk, your chair, and your friend. Solids are made up of molecules that group closely together and don't move around. Solids do have their own shape. The shape of a solid does not change when it's placed in a container.

7  Objects can sometimes change from one state of matter to another. For example, a liquid can evaporate and become a gas. A solid can melt and become a liquid, like when ice melts and turns into water. A liquid can freeze and become a solid, like when water freezes and becomes ice.

1.  Based on the passage and the illustration, which state of matter has the most spread out molecules?
   **A.** Gas
   **B.** Liquid
   **C.** Solid
   **D.** None. They're all equal.

2. How does the illustration help you better understand the passage?
   **A.** It corrects information that was wrong in the passage.
   **B.** It adds information about many more states of matter.
   **C.** It helps readers see and imagine the information in the passage, and adds new information about the ways that states of matter change.
   **D.** It makes the passage more fun to read.

3. Which state of matter has its own shape that does not change?
   **A.** Gas
   **B.** Liquid
   **C.** Solid
   **D.** All of the above.

4.  The passage explains that objects can change from one state of matter to another, like when melting causes a solid to become a liquid. The illustration has arrows that show how these changes can happen, including that freezing can cause a _____ to turn into a _____.

5.  Based on the information in the illustration, can a liquid turn into a gas? Explain your answer.

_____

_____

6.  Select the **TWO** types of molecules that move around.
   ☐  Gas
   ☐  Solid
   ☐  Liquid
   ☐  Condensation

## Passage 2: Moons of the Solar System

1    Did you know that Earth isn't the only planet with a moon? In fact, some planets have moons that are bigger than Earth's moon. Jupiter, for example, has 69 moons (that we know of), and some of them are massive.

2    Jupiter's four largest moons are Io, Europa, Ganymede, and Callisto. Europa is smaller than our moon, but the other three are larger. These four moons are very different from one another. For instance, Io is covered in volcanoes. Europa's surface is mostly water ice. Callisto is probably the most ancient, and it's covered in craters.

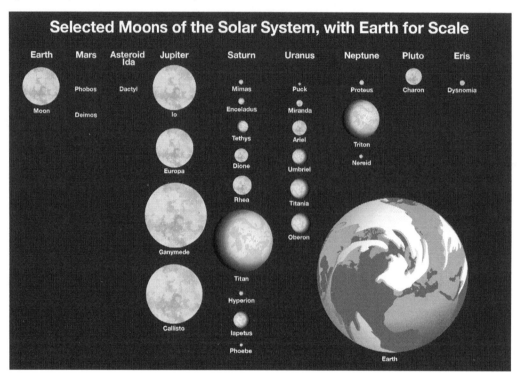

7. Based on the passage and the image, which of Jupiter's four largest moons is NOT bigger than Earth's moon?

    **A.** Io

    **B.** Europa

    **C.** Ganymede

    **D.** Callisto

8. Based on the image, what other planet has a moon that is much larger than Earth's moon?

    **A.** Mars

    **B.** Neptune

    **C.** Uranus

    **D.** Saturn

# DESCRIBE & MAKE CONNECTIONS IN TEXT

**RI.3.8 Describe the logical connection between particular sentences and paragraphs in a text (e.g., comparison, cause/effect, first/second/third in a sequence)**

*Directions: Read the passage and answer the questions that follow.*

## Passage 1: One Arm, All Heart

1    Bethany Hamilton was born in Hawaii in 1990. Bethany and her brothers all learned to surf at very young ages. By the young age of eight years old, Bethany Hamilton was a competitive surfer.

2    Bethany was home schooled so that she could pursue her passion of surfing. In 1999, Bethany became sponsored by the Hanalei Surf Company. As a competitor, Bethany was beating people who had been surfing much longer than she had and had much more experience.

3    In October of 2003, Bethany went surfing with her friend Alana, Alana's father, and Alana's brother at Tunnels Beach in Hawaii. Bethany was lying on her surfboard in the ocean when she suddenly felt an intense pressure on her arm while being pulled back and forth. Bethany noticed that the water around her was turning red, but she surprisingly didn't feel any pain. It was her friends who realized that her arm had been sundered to almost her shoulder.

4    Eventually, it was determined that Bethany was attacked by a 14-foot tiger shark. As a result of the attack, massive amounts of blood were extravasated from her arm, and Bethany had several surgeries. But, she was discharged from the hospital a few days later.

5    Despite losing her arm, Bethany pledged to get back to surfing as soon as possible. Just one month later, Bethany returned to the waves. In no time, she was back to competing and winning awards. Bethany Hamilton was back and better than ever.

1.  Why does the author include the information in Paragraph 2?
    **A.** To show that Bethany was a poor student
    **B.** To describe Bethany's passion for surfing
    **C.** To show Bethany was bad at surfing
    **D.** To introduce the problem

2. What is the relationship between Paragraph 3 and Paragraph 4?

    **A.** Paragraph 3 introduces a problem, and Paragraph 4 introduces the solution.

    **B.** Paragraph 3 shows a cause, and Paragraph 4 shows the effect.

    **C.** Paragraph 3 introduces a problem, and Paragraph 4 introduces a lesson..

    **D.** Paragraph 3 introduces the characters and setting, but Paragraph 4 introduces the problem and solution.

3. Why is Paragraph 5 included in the passage? Explain your reasoning using details from the passage.

_____

_____

_____

_____

_____

4. What are the effects of the shark attack? Choose all that apply.

☐ Bethany can no longer surf.

☐ Bethany undergoes many surgeries.

☐ Bethany loses her arm.

☐ Bethany has to stay in the hospital for several months.

☐ Bethany loses a lot of blood.

☐ Bethany makes a promise to herself to return to surfing

## Passage 2: Don't Give Up

1    Patricia Polacco was born on a farm in Michigan in 1944. She lived in Union City, Michigan with her parents and **beloved** grandparents. Patricia grew up in a storytelling family where she heard the most fascinating stories. Her babushka's (grandmother's) stories were some of her favorites.

2    Patricia's parents were divorced when she was just three years old. As a result, Patricia and her brother spent much of their childhood living in two places. They spent the school year in Oakland, California where their mother lived, and they spent the summers in Michigan where their father and grandparents lived.

3    Elementary school was very hard for Patricia. She tried very hard to learn how to read and write, but she just couldn't do it. The harder reading and writing became, the more Patricia concentrated on her drawing. She just loved to draw.

4    Throughout her childhood, Patricia was constantly teased and bullied. Children would call her names like "dumb" and "stupid." She especially hated to read out loud because she always made mistakes, and the teacher had to help her sound out every single word. Eventually, she despised going to school.

5    It wasn't until Patricia was fourteen years old that she learned how to read. One of Patricia's teachers recognized that she had a learning disability called **dyslexia.** Finally, Patricia was able to get the help she needed.

6    Now, Patricia Polacco is a famous writer of children's books. She has written several books such as *Thank You, Mr. Falker* and *The Keeping Quilt.* Many of her books tell about the stories her grandparents told her as a child. Her books also tell about her struggles with learning to read and how she was bullied. Patricia is a wonderful example that if we work hard and never give up, we can **accomplish** great things!

5.  Why is it important to mention in Paragraph 3 that school was very hard for Patricia?
    **A.** The author wanted us to infer that Patricia is a bad student.
    **B.** The author wanted us to infer that if Patricia tried harder in school, she would have learned how to read.
    **C.** It gives the reader interesting background information about Patricia.
    **D.** The author wanted us to understand that even though Patricia tried very hard in school, she still couldn't learn how to read.

6. How does the information in Paragraph 2 build on the information in Paragraph 1?

    **A.** Paragraph 1 introduces Patricia and Paragraph 2 tells more about her childhood.

    **B.** Paragraph 1 introduces the cause and Paragraph 2 presents the effect.

    **C.** Paragraph 2 presents the solution for the problem introduced in Paragraph 1.

    **D.** Paragraph 1 introduces why Patricia loves stories and Paragraph 2 explains the effect of this.

7. Even though Patricia has a learning disability, she is now a famous author of children's books. What are 2 factors that helped Patricia to become a famous author?

_____

_____

_____

_____

_____

8. Why does the author include Paragraph 4?

    **A.** To show that Patricia could have learned how to read if she tried harder

    **B.** To show why Patricia hated school

    **C.** To explain why Patricia gave up

    **D.** To show readers that bullying is bad

# COMPARE AND CONTRAST KEY POINTS IN TWO TEXTS

**RI.3.9 Compare and contrast the most important points and key details presented in two texts on the same topic.**

*Directions: Read the passages and answer the questions that follow.*

## Passage 1: Cell Phones Have No Place at School

1    School is a place to learn, and cell phones can prevent students from learning. For this reason, students should not bring cell phones to school.

2    Cell phones cause too much temptation. Students want to see if their friends are texting them, play fun games, watch videos, or check their social media apps. If students decide to look at their phones, they aren't able to pay attention to their assignments or to what the teacher is saying. They may miss important information.

3    Even if students do avoid the temptation to look at their cell phones, they may be distracted by thinking about checking their cell phones or wondering if someone is texting them.

4    Sometimes, students' cell phones go off in the middle of class, which can also be disruptive and distracting. Anything that can interrupt learning has no place in the classroom.

5    Lastly, some students use cell phones to share answers on assignments and tests. They may text each other answers or send one another pictures of assignments. Some students might also use their cell phones to look up answers for assignments and tests. When students cheat, they don't learn the information for themselves. This is another reason that cell phones can prevent kids from doing what they're supposed to be doing at school: learning.

## Passage 2: Should Cell Phones Be Allowed at School?

1    Many people disagree on the issue of whether or not cell phones should be allowed at school. There are convincing arguments on both sides.

2    It's true that cell phones can be very distracting for students. If students are too busy texting, playing games, or checking social media, they aren't as focused on their schoolwork as they should be. They could miss valuable information or not learn something that they will need later on. This can have a negative impact on their grades and on their education.

3    On the other hand, students may need to contact their parents after or even during school. What if an emergency happens? What if the student's after-school activity gets

cancelled and they need a parent to pick them up earlier? What if the parent needs to tell the student that someone else will be picking them up after school? Parents need to be able to get in contact with their children.

4    Students should be able to have their cell phones at school as a safety measure or in case they need to speak to their parents. But they shouldn't be allowed to have their cell phones out during class at all. Students must be responsible enough to have their cell phones at school without letting them distract from the purpose of attending school, which is learning.

1.  What is a key detail that is mentioned in both passages?
    **A.** Students may use cell phones to cheat on assignments or tests.
    **B.** Students need to be able to contact their parents in case of emergency.
    **C.** Cell phones can distract students from learning.
    **D.** Cell phones sometimes go off in class, causing a disruption.

2.  On which of the following statements would the author of Passage 1 and the author of Passage 2 disagree?
    **A.** Students may be distracted by texting and social media.
    **B.** Students shouldn't have their phones out in class at all.
    **C.** Cell phones should not be allowed to disrupt learning.
    **D.** Students should not be allowed to bring phones to school.

3. What is the main difference between Passage 1 and Passage 2? Explain.

_____

_____

_____

_____

_____

4.  Which of the following arguments is mentioned in Passage 1, but is not mentioned in Passage 2?
    **A.** Students may text each other answers or send one another pictures of assignments.
    **B.** Students could miss important information.
    **C.** Cell phones are distracting in school.
    **D.** The purpose of going to school is to learn.

5. List two arguments that are mentioned in Passage 2 but are not mentioned in Passage 1.

☐ Students may need to contact parents in case of an emergency.

☐ Students may be distracted by thinking about checking their cell phones or wondering if someone is texting them.

☐ When students cheat, they don't learn the information for themselves.

☐ Students should be able to have their cell phones at school as a safety measure or in case they need to speak to their parents.

6. The author of Passage 1 mentions that students may use their phones to cheat on assignments or tests. How would the author of Passage 2 most likely respond to this point?

**A.** That's why students shouldn't be allowed to have phones at school.

**B.** That's not as important as students being able to contact their parents.

**C.** This may be true, but students should not be allowed to have their cell phones out in class.

**D.** It's unlikely that cell phones would be used in this way.

7. Which passage do you agree with the most? Which arguments convinced you to agree with this passage?

_____

_____

_____

_____

_____

_____

8. Both authors agree that the purpose of school is _____.

**A.** Preparing students for adulthood.

**B.** Learning.

**C.** To understand when you should and should not use your phone during class.

**D.** Socializing.

# LANGUAGE

# DEMONSTRATE COMMAND OF GRAMMAR & USAGE

**L.1.1: Demonstrate command of the conventions of standard English grammar and usage when writing or speaking.**

1. What is the function of an adjective?
   - **A.** To describe a noun
   - **B.** To tell about an action
   - **C.** To name a person, place, or thing
   - **D.** To take the place of a noun

2. What is the adjective in the sentence below?
   The large dog ran across the street.
   - **A.** street
   - **B.** across
   - **C.** large
   - **D.** dog

3. What is the pronoun in the sentence below?
   Mr. White was scared of dogs, so he ran away.
   - **A.** Mr. White
   - **B.** he
   - **C.** dogs
   - **D.** ran

4. Choose the best adjective to fill in the blank.
   The horse was _____ than the dog.
   - **A.** big
   - **B.** bigger
   - **C.** biggest
   - **D.** more big

5. How would you change the noun bus to make it plural?
   - **A.** Add another -s
   - **B.** Double the -s, then add -es
   - **C.** Add an apostrophe and another -s
   - **D.** Add -es at the end

6. Complete the sentence below with the correct verb.
   I _____ to school yesterday.
   - **A.** walk
   - **B.** walked
   - **C.** walking
   - **D.** will walk

7. Complete the sentence below with the correct verb.
   We will _____ our favorite songs tomorrow in music class.
   - **A.** sing
   - **B.** sang
   - **C.** sung
   - **D.** singing

8. Choose the correct pronoun to agree with the antecedent in the sentence below.
Michael and Jose both ride _____ bikes to school.
   - **A.** his
   - **B.** our
   - **C.** their
   - **D.** him

9. Complete the sentence below with a coordinating conjunction.
For my birthday, I want to go to Disney World, _____ I want my best friends to come with me.
   - **A.** but
   - **B.** and
   - **C.** yet
   - **D.** nor

10. Complete the sentence below with a subordinating conjunction.
_____ school, John always goes to soccer practice.
   - **A.** Although
   - **B.** Whenever
   - **C.** While
   - **D.** After

11. What type of sentence is the sentence below?
Joey likes to read books, and he also likes to watch movies.
   - **A.** Simple
   - **B.** Compound
   - **C.** Complex
   - **D.** None of the above

12. What type of sentence is the sentence below?
Jenna also likes to read books, such as chapter books.
   - **A.** Simple
   - **B.** Compound
   - **C.** Complex
   - **D.** None of the above

# KNOW CAPITALIZATION, PUNCTUATION & SPELLING

**L.1.2 Demonstrate command of the conventions of standard English capitalization, punctuation, and spelling when writing.**

1. Which of the following titles is correctly capitalized?
    **A.** *The Lion, The Witch, And The Wardrobe*
    **B.** *The Lion, the Witch, And the Wardrobe*
    **C.** *The Lion, the Witch, and the Wardrobe*
    **D.** *the Lion, the Witch, and the Wardrobe*

2. Choose the address that uses commas correctly.
    **A.** 1520 King Street, Orlando, FL, 32825
    **B.** 1520 King Street Orlando, FL 32825
    **C.** 1520, King Street, Orlando, FL 32825
    **D.** 1520 King Street, Orlando, FL 32825

3. Which of the following sentences uses quotation marks and commas correctly?
    **A.** "I want to go home," said the little girl.
    **B.** "I want to go home", said the little girl.
    **C.** "I want to go home, said" the little girl.
    **D.** "I want to go home, said the little girl."

4. Which of the following sentences uses quotation marks and commas correctly?
    **A.** "After you finish your vegetables" Mom said, "you can have dessert."
    **B.** "After you finish your vegetables", Mom said "you can have dessert."
    **C.** "After you finish your vegetables," Mom said, "you can have dessert."
    **D.** "After you finish your vegetables Mom said," you can have dessert.

5. Complete the following sentence. The _____ car was shiny and red.
    **A.** mans
    **B.** man's
    **C.** mans'
    **D.** mans's

6. Complete the following sentence. Students were not allowed in the _____ lounge.
    **A.** teachers
    **B.** teacher's
    **C.** teachers'
    **D.** teachers's

7. Which of the following sentences is correct?
   **A.** It always wakes me up when my sister cries.
   **B.** It always wakes me up when my sister cry's.
   **C.** It always wakes me up when my sister crys.
   **D.** It always wakes me up when my sister crie's.

8. What suffix should be added to push to make it past tense?
   Yesterday, I _____ my sister on the swing.
   **A.** -ness
   **B.** -ly
   **C.** -ing
   **D.** -ed

9. What suffix should be added to sit to make it present tense?
   The class is _____ in the gym until the rain stops.
   **A.** -ness
   **B.** -ly
   **C.** -ing
   **D.** -ed

10. What suffix should be added to happy to refer to the state of being happy?
    The family was filled with love and _____ when the new baby was born.
    **A.** -ness
    **B.** -ly
    **C.** -ing
    **D.** -ed

# USE APPROPRIATE LANGUAGE CONVENTIONS

**L.2.3: Use knowledge of language and its conventions when writing, speaking, reading, or listening.**

1. It was finally the big day! Alexis was turning twelve.

   She expected her parents and friends to be as excited about her birthday as she was, but no one mentioned her birthday at breakfast. When Alexis got to school, she was sure her friends would run up to her and say, "Happy birthday". However, no one did.

   After school, Alexis went to soccer practice. She was sad and confused that her birthday had been forgotten. The soccer coach drove Alexis home from practice. Alexis was ready to go to sleep and forget the worst birthday ever. As soon as the coach opened the door, Alexis heard, "HAPPY BIRTHDAY!" and saw balloons, cake, presents, and all of her family and friends. She was definitely _____.

   Choose the word that **best** fills in the blank to describe how Alexis feels at the end of the passage?
   - **A.** sad
   - **B.** confused
   - **C.** upset
   - **D.** surprised

2. Starfish are truly _____ animals. Some of them have five arms, but others have as many as 40. If a starfish ever loses an arm, it can grow it back. Unlike most animals, starfish don't have blood or bones.

   Choose the word that **best** fits in the blank to complete the sentence.
   - **A.** beautiful
   - **B.** unique
   - **C.** boring
   - **D.** common

3. In a village long ago, there lived a massive dragon. He was taller than the tallest castle in the kingdom, and he could breathe fire for miles. Many brave knights had tried to defeat the dragon, but no one could do it. There was a rumor that the dragon was going to destroy the entire village with his fiery breath. All of the villagers were so _____ that they had nightmares for weeks.

   Choose the word that best fits in the blank to describe how the villagers feel about the dragon.
   - **A.** excited
   - **B.** terrified
   - **C.** nervous
   - **D.** gloomy

4. Many people believe that Michael Jordan is the greatest basketball player ever. But when he was fifteen-years-old, he tried out for his high school basketball team and didn't make it. After finding out he didn't make the team, Jordan went home, went into his bedroom, and cried.

   Jordan could have given up. He could have decided he would never be a great basketball player. Instead, he used not making the team as _____. It made him work even harder. Whenever he didn't feel like practicing his shot or lifting weights, Jordan closed his eyes. He remembered how he felt when his name wasn't on the team list. That was enough _____ to keep going. The next year, Jordan made the high school basketball team and quickly became their best player.

   Choose the word that best fits the blanks to complete the sentences.
   - **A.** motivation
   - **B.** disappointment
   - **C.** happiness
   - **D.** defeat

5. A big scoop of ice cream fell off Melissa's ice cream cone. She felt _____ as she watched her ice cream land on the grass.

   Which word best completes the sentence and describes the girl's feelings?
   - **A.** tired
   - **B.** confused
   - **C.** sad
   - **D.** worried

6. What sentence does NOT describe the ocean?
   **A.** The ocean contains waves, big and small.
   **B.** I love playing in the ocean.
   **C.** The ocean is a huge body of salt water.
   **D.** The ocean is a large area of sea

7. Which sentence best describes a happy puppy?
   **A.** We could hear him whining from the other room.
   **B.** He was running faster than the speed of light.
   **C.** He growled like a lion and showed his teeth.
   **D.** He jumped around like a bunny rabbit, wagging his tail back and forth.

8. What does this phrase "You crack me up," mean?
   **A.** You make them laugh.
   **B.** You broke something.
   **C.** You hurt them.
   **D.** You made them cry.

9. What does the phrase "to go the extra mile" mean?"
   **A.** Walk a long distance.
   **B.** Keep running after everyone else stops.
   **C.** Do more than what is expected or required.
   **D.** Try your best.

10. What does the following sentence mean?

Miguel stayed home from school because he was feeling a little under the weather.

   **A.** Miguel stayed home from school because it was too cold.
   **B.** Miguel stayed home from school because he didn't feel like going anywhere.
   **C.** Miguel stayed home from school because it might rain.
   **D.** Miguel stayed home from school because he felt sick.

# DETERMINE MEANING OF UNKNOWN WORD/S IN CONTEXT

**L.3.4: Determine or clarify the meaning of unknown and multiple-meaning words and phrases based on grade 3 reading and content, choosing flexibly from a range of strategies.**

1. Fish, whales, and dolphins are aquatic animals.
   Based on the context clues, what do you think the word **aquatic** means?
      **A.** Large
      **B.** Small
      **C.** Water
      **D.** Gentle

2. Mom had to **sterilize** the baby's bottle to make sure it was clean.
   What does the word **sterilize** mean in this sentence?
      **A.** Clean
      **B.** Buy
      **C.** Find
      **D.** Look at

3. Elephants and hippos have a **pewter** color to their skin.
   What does the word **pewter** mean in this sentence? How do the context clues help you?

   _____

   _____

   _____

4. Our waitress was in a bad mood and was not very **cordial** to us.
   What does the word **cordial** mean in this sentence?
      **A.** Rude
      **B.** Talkative
      **C.** Polite
      **D.** Bored

5. Jimmy was terrible at crossword puzzles, but his sister Julie was very **adept** at them.
   What do you think the word **adept** means in this sentence?
      **A.** Terrible
      **B.** Good
      **C.** Okay
      **D.** Interested

6. The base word **agree** means to have the same opinion about something. What do you think the word **agreeable** means?

    **A.** Happy
    **B.** Argumentative
    **C.** Not able to share the same opinion
    **D.** Able to share the same opinion

7. The base word **complete** means finished. What does the word **incomplete** mean?

 

 

 

8. What is the difference in meaning between the words **preheat** and **reheat**?

 

 

 

9. What root word do the following words have in common: **Section, bisect, dissect**

 

 

 

    What does the word **bisect** mean?

 

 

 

10. What suffix should be added to happy to refer to the state of being happy?
The family was filled with love and _____ when the new baby was born.

    **A.** -ness
    **B.** -ly
    **C.** -ing
    **D.** -ed

# UNDERSTAND WORD RELATIONSHIPS AND NUANCES IN MEANING

**L.3.5: Demonstrate understanding of word relationships and nuances in word meanings.**

1. What does the bold phrase mean in the following sentence?
   After Chloe and her best friend Naya had a big argument, Chloe wanted to **take steps** to fix their friendship.
   - **A.** Go for a walk
   - **B.** Take action
   - **C.** Run away
   - **D.** Walk to Naya's house

2. What does the bold phrase mean in the following sentence?
   Max was bigger and stronger than his brother Peter, so Max had the **upper hand** in competitions like wrestling.
   - **A.** The advantage
   - **B.** His hand was on top
   - **C.** His hand was bigger
   - **D.** The disadvantage

3. Is the following sentence figurative or literal? Explain why.
   After practice, Sarah was so hungry she could eat a horse.

   _____

   _____

   _____

4. Is the following sentence figurative or literal? Explain why.
   The boy was as tall as a giraffe.

   _____

   _____

   _____

5. Which word has a similar meaning to **annoyed**?
   - **A.** Amused
   - **B.** Aggravated
   - **C.** Joyful
   - **D.** Confused

6. Which word is similar in meaning to **massive**?

    **A.** Short

    **B.** Long

    **C.** Huge

    **D.** Tiny

7. Which word means the opposite of **fascinated**?

    **A.** Scared

    **B.** Entertained

    **C.** Happy

    **D.** Bored

8. Which word could replace the bold word to describe the situation in more detail.
   The boy happily **walked** home.

    **A.** ran

    **B.** skipped

    **C.** stomped

    **D.** tiptoed

9. Which sentence seems to suggest that Anthony is *most* upset? Explain why.

    **A.** Anthony was mad.

    **B.** Anthony was furious.

    **C.** Anthony was displeased.

    **D.** Anthony was irritated.

10. Which sentence has a more positive implication?

    **A.** The girl frowned.

    **B.** The girl smirked.

    **C.** The girl laughed.

    **D.** The girl stared.

11. Find the synonym for the bold word in the sentence below.
    The **sluggish** turtle finished the race last.

    **A.** Slow

    **B.** Fast

    **C.** Speedy

    **D.** Friendly

# KNOW ACADEMIC/DOMAIN-SPECIFIC WORDS

**L.3.6: Acquire and use accurately conversational, general academic, and domain specific words and phrases as found in grade appropriate texts, including those that signal spatial and temporal relationships (e.g., After dinner that night we went looking for them).**

1. In which of the following classes would you most likely use the word "simile?"
   **A.** Math
   **B.** English/Language Arts
   **C.** Music
   **D.** Science

2. Which of the following words means "the total amount when adding two or more numbers?"
   **A.** Perimeter
   **B.** Area
   **C.** Sum
   **D.** Estimate

3. In which class would you most likely learn about "amphibians?"
   **A.** Math
   **B.** English/Language Arts
   **C.** Music
   **D.** Science

4. What does it mean if your teacher asks you to "use context clues" to figure out the meaning of a word?
   **A.** Look up the word in the dictionary.
   **B.** Ask your friend what the word means.
   **C.** Figure out what the word means based on the information in the sentence.
   **D.** Raise your hand and ask the teacher for the meaning of the word.

5. In which class would you most likely learn about "antecedents?"
   **A.** Math
   **B.** English/Language Arts
   **C.** Music
   **D.** Science

6. What does the word "contrast" mean?

    **A.** Describe similarities between two or more things.

    **B.** Describe differences between two or more things.

    **C.** A word that has the same meaning as another word.

    **D.** List events in order.

7. Choose the most accurate definition of solar system.

    **A.** The planets and moons that orbit the sun.

    **B.** The organs and glands in the body that are responsible for digestion.

    **C.** The process of water circulating between the oceans, atmosphere, and land.

    **D.** The different types of clouds, including cumulus and cirrus.

8. Select the word or phrase that best completes the sentence below.

The student who was _____ me in line kept stepping on the back of my shoes.

    **A.** in front of

    **B.** behind

    **C.** next to

    **D.** to the right of

9. Select the word or phrase that best completes the sentence below.

We had to wake up early enough to get breakfast _____ school.

    **A.** in the meantime

    **B.** during

    **C.** after

    **D.** before

10. Select the word or phrase that best completes the sentence below.

The plane flew far _____ my head.

    **A.** outside

    **B.** above

    **C.** parallel to

    **D.** in front of

# ANSWER EXPLANATIONS

# READING LITERATURE

## RL.1.1 Ask & Answer Questions Using Text Evidence

1. Part A- **C.** The man believes the cheeses will meet him at the marketplace, which is what he tells them to do when he lets them go.

Part B- **A.** Once the man believes that the cheeses can find their way to the market alone, he states: "Well, then, if you can go to market alone, so can the other cheeses, and I will send them along after you." This statement proves that the man is confident the cheeses will find their way and meet him there.

2. **B.** When the author tell us that the cheeses roll into different bushes, but the man doesn't notice this, we begin to realize that the cheeses will never make their way all the way down to market.

3. After the first cheese escapes, the man says, "So you can run to the market alone, can you? I wish I had known that before. It would have saved me the trouble of carrying you. Well then, if you can go to market alone, so can the other cheeses, and I will send them along after you" (Paragraph 3). As long as students identify any segment of this quote and are able to explain their thinking, the answer should be considered correct. This quote shows that the man is tired of carrying the cheeses and that he believes the first cheese escaped to go to the market. For these reasons, he lets the other cheeses go as well.

4. **B.** Since it is already evening and the cheeses haven't arrived, and since the title of the passage is "The Cheeses That Ran Away," it can be inferred that the man will never find his cheeses. Also, we know that when he rolled the cheeses down the hill, the man didn't realize that some of the cheeses rolled into bushes instead.

5. The man's opinion is that the kettle will follow him home. He gives the kettle directions to where he lives (para 5), and he tells his wife that the kettle is on its way, and "be along in good time." (para 6).

The wife disagrees with the husband and doesn't believe the kettle will arrive at the home. She asks the husband where he left it and "hurries off to get it." The passage also states, "She was not so sure about its coming as he was."

6. In Paragraph 2, the man realizes that the kettle has three legs, while he only has two. This leads him to the decision that the kettle should carry him instead of the other way around.

7. **B.** Both the cheeses and the kettle disobey their owners. The cheeses are told to go to the market and run away instead. The kettle is told to go to the man's home and refuses to walk.

8. Part A- **C.** The woman doesn't think the kettle will come home, which is why she repeatedly asks the man where he has left the kettle.

Part B- **B.** The woman goes to get the kettle and bring it home. After asking her husband where the kettle is located, she "hurries off to get it."

## RL.1. 2. Recount Stories & Determine Theme

1. (2) The Grasshopper says there's no need to worry about winter because they have plenty of food at present.

(5) The Grasshopper has no food in the winter and begins to die of starvation, while the ants continue to eat the grain and corn they collected in the summer.

2. Answers may vary. A main lesson is that you should always work hard and prepare for difficult times during the good times. (This is conveyed as the Grasshopper refuses to prepare for the winter and faces the consequences, while the Ant diligently prepares and has plenty of food during the winter.)

3. **D.** We see that the Grasshopper should have prepared like the Ant because the Grasshopper has no food and is starving.

4. The Grasshopper says that there is plenty of food right now, and later he says that winter is still many days away.

5. Answers may vary. One lesson is to listen to your parents. (Icarus is told by his father not to fly too close to the sun, but he ignores the warning and falls into the ocean.)

6. **C.** Icarus doesn't listen to his father. The wax begins to melt, the seagull feathers begin to fall off, and Icarus falls into the ocean and drowns. This teaches the lesson that Icarus should have listened to Daedalus, and children should listen to their parents.

7. **B.** The beginning of the passage states that Daedalus and Icarus are imprisoned because Daedalus is a very talented inventor, and King Minos wants Daedalus to only make inventions for him.

8. **D.** Only the title "The Disobedient Son" does a good job of summarizing the story and conveying its overall message. "Flying," "The Inventor and his Inventions," and "The Greedy King Minos" are too specific and not representative of the story as a whole.

## RL.1.3 Describe Characters & Explain Their Actions

1. **B.** They both have positive attitudes. Each time a problem happens during the camp out, Jessica and Tia do their best to stay positive and still enjoy themselves.

2. **A.** She's a good friend. The passage also says that Tia didn't want Jessica to feel bad about forgetting the marshmallows, which shows she cares about her friend's feelings.

3. Answers may vary. Students should say that they would or would not like to be friends with Tia and Jessica, and they should provide at least one detail from the passage to support their response. For example, students might say that they would like to be friends with the girls because they seem nice (like when Tia didn't want Jessica to feel bad) and try to make the best of any situation (like when they try to enjoy the smores even though they aren't the same).

4. **2nd and 4th Choice.** Both of these details show the girls being flexible by adapting to the problems that occur on the camp out.

5. At the beginning, Lauren doesn't like raking leaves. (She pouts and sighs while dragging the rake "for what felt like the hundredth time.") After spending the day raking leaves with Drew, Lauren learns to enjoy raking. (She smiles when her dad says raking leaves should be her chore from now on and says, "Raking leaves isn't so bad."). There are other details that could be added, but these are some of the main ones.

6. Part A- **A.** Like Tia and Jessica in the first passage, Drew can make the best of a bad situation. He makes raking leaves fun by playing games and having a positive attitude about raking.

Part B- **C.** Drew responds enthusiastically when Lauren asks if he's sure about helping with the leaves, and he immediately suggests a way to make raking more fun.

7. Drew is a good friend because he volunteers to help Lauren with raking the leaves, and he tries to cheer her up and make her task more fun with games like leaf jumping and races.

8. Lauren: She doesn't like raking leaves.

Supporting Detail: She sighs and pouts while raking the leaves, and she can't believe that anyone would volunteer to help with something so boring.

Drew: He doesn't mind raking leaves.

Supporting Detail: He volunteers to help Lauren.

When she asks if he's sure, he enthusiastically says, "Of course!" Immediately, he begins finding ways to make raking the leaves more fun.

## RL.2.4 Determine Word Meaning In Context

1. **A.** The author is nervous. The text says that the author is worried, and it also says that the author has practiced for weeks. We know that she's prepared, but she's still nervous that something might go wrong.

2. Fell asleep. Readers can guess that "dozed off" means fell asleep because the text says that Josie was bored and tired.

3. The phrases "straight down" and "into the water" tell readers that plunge means to fall down. The fact that the bridge is old and Peter must walk carefully are additional hints.

4. The author compares his struggles in math class to climbing a mountain. He says, "We all have challenges in life. We all have our mountains to climb. For me, it's math class." He also talks about working hard and eventually "reaching the top."

5. **A.** Fast. Liz wins every race, and it's never even close. This tells us that Liz is very fast.

6. **C.** Courage. Peter is the only one who is brave enough to go into Old Man Frank's yard; everyone else is too scared.

7. **B.** "...and listened for the sound of Old Man Frank yelling." The fact that they are listening for a noise shows readers that "caught our breath" means to be silent and wait.

8. Answers may vary. There are several clues: the phrase, "Except he wasn't yelling" shows that the boys were wrong in their assumptions (guesses) about Old Man Frank. The sentence, "It seemed like he wasn't so scary after all," also indicates that the boys had guessed incorrectly. Details like Old Man Frank asking friendly questions and telling stories about his childhood provide additional clues.

## RL.2.5 Identify & Understand Parts Of Texts

1. **B.** A poem. Poems are divided into stanzas like stories are divided into paragraphs.

2. **B.** Scene. Plays are divided into scenes like stories are divided into paragraphs.

3. **C.** Line breaks are used to enhance ideas and meaning in a poem.

4. At the beginning of the story, so readers

understand where the story takes place and who the characters are. It would be confusing if setting and characters were introduced later in the story.

5. At the end, because the story is over once the problem is solved. There's no reason to continue the story when there's no problem to solve.

6. **B.** There are four stanzas in this poem

7. **C.** The little master should appreciate that the sheep grows wool that will be used to make the master's clothing.

8. **B.** These lines show that when spring is over, the sheep's wool is cut to warm the master through the cold winter. While the sheep may seem lazy in the spring, he benefits the master in the winter.

## RL.2.6 Identify Point Of View of Self & Author/Characters

1. **C.** Point of view is who is narrating or telling the story. It's the perspective from which the story is told.

2. **B.** Third-person point of view is when a character is not an active participant in the story. Words like "he," "she," and "they" are used.

3. Part A- **C.** A puppy is the narrator of the story.

Part B- **B.** The man who brings the puppy home. It isn't clear that the narrator is a puppy until the man says, "Hi, little puppy!"

4. **A.** The story is told from the first-person point of view. The narrator, the puppy, is an active participant in the story, and he uses words like "I."

5. The author makes the reader feel sad and worried for the puppy. Details like the puppy being cold, people honking and yelling at the puppy, and the puppy being hungry create this feeling.

6. **C.** The puppy is cold because of the rain, and he's trying to find shelter.

7. Part A- **B** "…but she didn't look very happy." This quote shows that the woman will allow the puppy to stay at her house, but she doesn't truly want him to be there.

Part B- **A.** The woman doesn't know that the dog is homeless. This might make her feel more sorry for the puppy and want to help him.

8. All of the other human characters in the story don't like the dog and don't want to help him. People honk at the puppy, and someone yells, "Get out of the way!" Another man tells the puppy, "Get lost!" Susie, the man's wife, says, "Are you crazy?" when the man brings the puppy home. Only the man is nice to the puppy, calling him cute, asking if he has anywhere to go, and bringing him home.

## RL.3.7 Identify How Illustrations Convey Information

1. Answers may vary. Nathan and Julie got off the school bus, and they're excited about having a great first day of school.

2. Answers may vary. Nathan and Julie seem like they feel happy in this picture. The twins are smiling. They are walking with big strides, or possibly skipping. The text says that they're finally in the same class, their new teacher seems nice, and most of their best friends are in the class too. It also says that they're confident third grade will be a good year.

3. Some of the clues that the author gives that prove Nathan and Julie feel like they will have a great year in third grade is: they've never been in the same class before, but they are this year; their new teacher seems very nice, and many of their best friends are also in their class. In the pictures, both Nathan and Julie are smiling, they're holding hands, and they're walking with big strides or skipping. This shows they are confident about having a great third grade year.

4. **B.** In comparison to the person in the photo, this image emphasizes the dog's massive size (which is described in the text).

5. **D.** As the text also explains, this image shows that the dog is sweet and loving. His hands are on the girl's shoulders, almost like a hug. It looks like he's being very gentle despite his size.

6. The purpose of this image is to help readers visualize the information in the text (or to further emphasize the information in the text). In the text, the writer explains that although her dog is huge, he's very sweet and loving. The image shows that the dog is enormous as well, but it also shows that the dog is loving and gentle. He's not mean or scary, as some people assume based on his size.

7. Answers may vary. The boy looks as though he's feeling scared or nervous. Evidence that the boy looks scared or nervous is that his eyes are wide, his mouth is curved and his teeth are showing, his hands are up to defend himself, the bee is looking at him angrily, and it looks as though several more bees are coming out of the beehive.

## RL. 3.9 Compare & Contrast Narratives

1. Both the farmer and the dog are greedy and want more than they already have. The farmer wants more than one golden egg each day, and the dog wants a bigger bone. They both attempt to gain more and instead lose what they already had (the goose for the farmer and the bone for the dog).

2. Part A- **B.** The golden goose and the farmer live on a farm.

Part B- **A.** The dog is walking past a river when he thinks his reflection is another dog with a bigger bone.

3. Part A- **D.** Both characters should have been grateful for what they have instead of being greedy. Then the farmer would still have his golden goose and the dog would still have his bone. Instead, both characters end up with nothing.

Part B- **D.** The fact that the farmer's goose dies at the end of the story develops the theme that the farmer should have been grateful for what he had instead of being greedy.

4. The farmer's decision: To cut open the goose for more eggs

The result: There are no eggs inside the goose, and the goose dies.

The dog's decision: To jump into the river in an attempt to get a bigger bone from the "other dog" (which was really his reflection).

The result: The dog has to frantically swim to shore, loses his bone, and of course does not get a bigger bone either.

5. **A.** In both stories, the conflict occurs as the result of the main characters not being satisfied with what they have.

6. The farmer cut open his goose in hopes of getting more golden eggs. The story explains that the goose only laid one golden egg each day, and the farmer was getting impatient. He wanted more eggs and more money, so he decided to cut open the goose.

7. The dog jumped into the river because he thought his reflection was another dog with a bigger bone than the one he had been given by the butcher. The passage explains that if the dog had thought for a moment, he might have realized his mistake. Instead, he impulsively jumped into the river to try to get the bigger bone from the dog.

8. All options show the farmer and dog are different except the 4th and the 6th option, which contain information that is either incorrect or not in the passage.

## READING INFORMATION

### RI.1.1 Ask & Answer Questions Using Text Evidence

1. **B.** The starfish is not a fish. The passage explains that scientists are trying to change the name to "sea star" since starfish are not actually fish.

2. **C.** The passage mentions that starfish use their colors as camouflage and to scare off predators and that starfish have hard, bony skin that can protect them from predators. However, starfish don't have sharp spikes on their arms.

3. Answers may vary. Some possible answers are:
1) The starfish doesn't have blood or brains.

2) The starfish can regrow its arms and even grow a whole new starfish from its arm.

3) Starfish have one eye on the tip of each arm and can't see color.

4. The text says that many starfish have 5 arms, but some species of starfish have 10, 20, or even 40 arms.

5. **(2)** The virus makes the starfish weak.

**(4)** The starfish develops white sores on its body.

**(5)** The arms sometimes rip off and walk away.

6. **A.** The beginning of the passage states that starfish were dying out "across North America."

7. Part A- **B.** The virus normally affects just one or two species, but now over 20 species have been affected.

Part B- **C.** Scientists think the virus may be spreading more quickly because there are so many starfish packed into small areas.

8. The passage says scientists will continue to study the parvovirus. They want to stop the virus, but if they can't do that, they want to learn more about the virus so they can prevent an outbreak like this one in the future.

### RI.1.2 Determine Main Idea & Explain Key Details

1. **B.** The main idea of this passage is that potato chips were an accidental invention. The passage goes on to provide details of exactly how potato chips were accidentally invented.

2. Answers may vary. Possibilities include, "George Crum's customers complained that his fried potatoes were too thick and bland, so he tried to make disgusting fried potatoes that were too thin and too salty," or, "Instead, the customers loved

**ANSWER EXPLANATIONS**

the fried potatoes, and soon everyone was talking about the tasty new invention of potato chips." Students may also cite the first or last lines of the text, which specifically mention that potato chips were an accidental invention.

3. **C.** This sentence supports the idea that potato chips were not intentionally invented. Instead, they originated from a hotel chef trying to prank some customers who didn't like his food.

4. **D.** The title "Potato Chips: A Happy Accident" represents the main idea of this passage well. The other three choices focus on specific details or aspects of the text that don't represent the text as a whole.

5. **A.** This passage focuses on the idea that although people long believed that Abner Doubleday invented baseball, we don't know who truly invented the sport.

6. Answers may vary. Possibilities include, "Until 2011, popular legend was that a man named Abner Doubleday invented baseball," and, "The rumor was so popular that the Baseball Hall of Fame was opened in Cooperstown, New York, where baseball was supposedly invented." These statements support the idea that the legend of Abner Doubleday was very popular. The following details support the idea that Doubleday didn't invent baseball, and we don't know who did: Historian John Thorn published a book explaining that baseball was played long before 1939, various versions of the game existed in New York, Philadelphia, Massachusetts, and Britain, and John Thorn says the question of who invented baseball is one we may never be able to answer.

7. **D.** The information about Abner Doubleday being a Civil War general does not support or relate to the main idea of the passage (the invention of baseball).

8. **C.** The passage explains that we'll probably never know who invented baseball (mostly because so many variations of it were played in many different locations).

## RI.1.3 Describe & Understand Relationships Between Ideas

1. **B.** People believed that the *Titanic* was unsinkable and that nothing bad could happen to the ship, so they didn't have as many lifeboats as they should have.

2. **A.** The passage explains that many historians think the captain of the ship was trying to beat the time of another ship, the *Olympic*.

3. Students should include any two possible details:

People believed that the *Titanic* was "the safest ship ever" and it was unsinkable, warnings about icebergs were ignored, the captain was traveling too fast in an effort to beat the time of another ship, and there were only enough lifeboats for half the passengers and crew.

4. Because people believed the *Titanic* was so safe, they made poor decisions. They believed that nothing bad could happen to the ship, so there weren't enough lifeboats on board for everyone. If they hadn't believed that the ship was unsinkable, they might have taken the warnings about icebergs more seriously. The captain might have also traveled more slowly and safely. As a result, damages to the ship and the loss of passengers and crew was much worse than it might have been if people had been more cautious.

5. The entire city was constructed of wood, firefighters were exhausted because of the 20 fires that had occurred the previous week, and firefighters were sent to the wrong neighborhood at first.

6. **C.** The firefighters were sent to the wrong neighborhood at first, so the fire was out of control by the time they finally arrived at the O'Leary home.

7. **B.** The people of Chicago blamed Mrs. O'Leary and her cow. The passage explains that even though Mrs. O'Leary told reporters she was sleeping when the fire started, the newspapers reported that she was milking the cow and the cow kicked over a lantern, starting the destructive fire.

8. When the city was reconstructed, architects built some of the first skyscrapers. The population and economy grew, and the city of Chicago became a great city.

9. Mrs. O'Leary barely left her house after the Chicago Fire. She avoided other people because almost the entire city blamed her for the fire and felt angry about the destruction she had supposedly caused.

10. **B.** The fire finally stopped two days later when it rained.

11. Both passages are about accidents or disasters that are thought to have happened because of a person's actions. The *Titanic* passage reveals that historians believe that the captain of the *Titanic* made the ship go too fast for icy waters, which resulted in the crash. In the Great Chicago Fire passage, the newspapers reported that Ms O'Leary knocked over a lamp which started the fire. Also, in both passages, some people lost their lives because

the thing/person(s) expected to save them did not. In the case of the *Titanic,* there were not enough lifeboats on the ship to get all the people to safety. In the Great Chicago Fire, the firefighters were not able to put the fire out (the rain eventually put the fire out), and hundreds of people died.

## RI.2.4 Determine Domain-Specific Word Meaning in Context

1. **A.** We know that prevalent means "common" because the next sentence mentions that people visit from all over to see the "many" cacti in these states.

2. **A** succulent is a plant that can store water. The passage explains that cacti can store water in their stems, roots, and leaves and can survive without rain for up to a year.

3. **B.** Hue means color. This part of the passage is about how most cacti are green, but some are slightly different colors like brownish and bluish.

4. **D.** Imagine. The sentence suggests that "picture" is a synonym for "envision," so readers can infer that "imagine" is a synonym as well.

5. **A** chocolatier is a person who makes chocolate. The passage states, "To transform these bitter cocoa beans into delicious chocolate, chocolatiers have to first dry out the beans." This suggests that the chocolatier is the person who takes the cocoa beans and makes them into chocolate.

6. **C.** In this sentence, "the finished product" refers to the chocolate. The cocoa beans and cocoa nibs occur earlier in the process. The very next sentence starts with the words, "The chocolate," which shows us that the author used the phrase "the finished product" to refer to the chocolate. Later, a candy bar is introduced as one treat that can be made with the chocolate.

7. **B.** The cocoa liquor and cocoa butter are removed from the cocoa nibs.

8. **A** and **C.** The chocolate bar travels from one place to another to get to the consumer, and it also undergoes a long process as it is transformed from cocoa beans into chocolate. "A fun trip or vacation" or 'ocean voyage' doesn't

make sense in this context, and although "hard work" is required to make the chocolate, it's NOT a definition for the word "journey."

## RI.2.5 Use Text Features & Search Tools

1. **C.** Headings are intended to help readers find the main idea of sections in order to locate information easily.

2. **B.** Bold text is used to indicate key words and phrases and draw the reader's attention to this essential information.

3. **D.** This section contains information about rock features, including stalactites, which are rock formationss that hang from the ceiling.

4. **B.** Bats are cave creatures, which are discussed under the heading "Cave Creatures."

5. **A.** Paragraphs. The key difference between solutional caves and sea caves is provided in paragraphs (Paragraphs 4 and 5), including the facts that, solutional caves are formed by rainfall and chemical processes, while sea caves are formed by erosion.

6. Part A- **D.** The article explains that sea caves form when sea cliffs are eroded by waves and tides.

Part B- **B** and **C.** Readers could immediately go to the heading "Types of Caves" to find information about sea caves. They could then quickly locate the definition using the bolded text.

7. **D.** Searching "Cave types" would lead to information about all the different kinds of caves. Searching "Solutional caves" would only provide information on one type of cave rather than on many different types.

8. **A.** A glossary is an alphabetical list of words with definitions.

## RI.2.6 Identify Point Of View of Self & Author

1. **1st and 3rd Choices.** These sentences best express the author's overall point of view: that exercise offers many excellent benefits. The other two options are specific details that support this viewpoint.

2. Part A - **C.** The author might agree with options A and B, but we don't know this information based on the text. D is incorrect because the author points out that you don't have to go to the gym to experience the benefits of exercise.

Part B- **D.** This piece of evidence includes information about exercise benefitting both the body and the mind.

3. Answers will vary. Correct answers will include an explanation of why students agree or disagree with the viewpoint stated in the article (that exercising is beneficial and important). They will state specific details from the passage and explain how they influenced the student's point of view (to agree or disagree with the author's viewpoint) Example:" I agree with the viewpoint that exercise is important for your body and mind. When you exercise, you can maintain a healthy body weight and at the same time, you will feel happier and more relaxed. It also helps prevent diseases that harm your health, like diabetes." The passage contains less evidence to use if a student disagrees with the author.

4. **C.** The author's point of view is that too much TV is harmful. The other details are included in the article, but they're too specific and don't represent the author's overall viewpoint.

5. **A.** "Don't overdo it," best summarizes the author's point of view about television. The other words don't give us enough information to express the author's viewpoint.

6. Part A- **C.** A is incorrect because the author believes TV is fine in moderation. B is never mentioned in the passage. D is too much of a generalization. The author does say that kids who witness bad behaviors on TV may imitate it, but does not claim that all kids who watch TV behave badly.

Part B- **B.** This quote shows that the author believes activities like reading and spending time with family are healthier than watching television.

7. Answers ma vary. Correct answers will state whether the student agrees or disagrees with the author's viewpoint (that too much television harms children) and explain the reasoning behind this stance. Student reasoning for whether they agree or disagree must be supported with information from the passage. For this reason, it makes it difficult for students to disagree with the author's viewpoint. The passage is filled with facts supporting why children need to watch less television. A typical child will likely disagree with the article because they like to watch television or because they disagree that watching television is unhealthy or can lead to violent behavior. However, these are opinions based on the student's thinking and not based on the facts from the article.

8. The title of the article is "Turn Off the TV." Immediately, readers understand that the author may think television (or too much television) is bad, since the author is encouraging people to stop watching.

## RI.3.7 Use & Understand Information In Illustrations

1. **A.** The passage explains that gas molecules are spread out, and the image also shows that they are by far the most spread out molecules among the states of matter.

2. **C.** The illustration helps readers visualize the information that is provided in the text, and, in this case, also adds new information (with the arrows and labels) about the ways that states of matter change.

3. **C.** The shape of a solid does not change, even if it's placed in a container.

4. Liquid, Solid. The arrow and "Freezing" label on the image indicates that a liquid can change into a solid through the process of freezing.

5. Based on the illustration, it looks like a liquid can turn into a gas. There are arrows pointing from the liquid to the gas with the label "evaporation".

6. **1st and 3rd Choices.** Gas and liquid molecules move around, but solid molecules don't. Condensation is not a type of molecule.

7. **B.** Europa is the only one of Jupiter's four largest moons that is not larger than Earth's moon.

8. **D.** Saturn's moon Titan is much larger than

Earth's moon. Neptune's moon Triton looks close in size to Earth's moon, but Titan is much bigger, making Saturn the better answer.

## RI.3.8 Describe & Make Connections In Text

1. **B.** The information in Paragraph 2 introduces the reader to Bethany's passion for surfing. The author states that "Bethany was home schooled so that she could pursue her passion for surfing." It also describes how Bethany is able to beat people who have surfed longer than her, so we can infer that she works hard and really enjoys surfing.

2. **B.** Paragraph 3 introduces the cause which is Bethany is attacked by the shark. Paragraph 4 introduces the effects of shark attack such as: she has to go to the hospital, she loses a lot of blood, she loses her arm,and she has to have a lot of surgeries.

3. Paragraph 5 shows us that Bethany did not stop surfing just because she lost her arm. It also shows us that Bethany refused to give up. Students may include any of the following details to support their answer: "Despite losing her arm, Bethany pledged to get back to surfing as soon as possible." Also, just one month after the attack, Bethany returned to surfing. Lastly, she continued to be a great surfer with one arm because she won awards and competitions.

4. **2nd, 3rd, 5th & 6th Choices.** Students should select the following answer choices: Bethany undergoes many surgeries, Bethany loses her arm, Bethany loses a lot of blood, and Bethany makes a promise to herself to return to surfing. The 4th answer choice, Bethany has to stay in the hospital for several months, is incorrect because the passage states that Bethany is released from the hospital a few days later.

5. **D.** In Paragraph 3, we learn that school is very hard for Patricia. We learn that she tried to learn how to read and write, but she just couldn't do it. There are no clues in this paragraph that Patricia is a bad student or that she could have tried harder. It is not interesting background information about Patricia because it is important for the reader to understand that Patricia still couldn't read or write, despite trying very hard in school.

6. **A.** In Paragraph 1, we are introduced to Patricia and her family. In Paragraph 2, we learn more about Patricia and her family. We learn that her parents get divorced, and we learn that Patricia has to live in two separate places. There is no cause/effect or problem/solution relationship between Paragraph 1 and Paragraph 2.

7. Answers may vary. Several factors have helped Patricia to become a famous author. In Paragraph 5, we learn that she is diagnosed with dyslexia and finally gets the help she needs. Therefore, Patricia learns how to read. In Paragraph 6, the author explains that Patricia is a wonderful example of what can happen if we work hard and never give up. Students may also include that Patricia still went to school and worked hard even though she was bullied. Students should include any 2 of these reasons.

8. **B.** Paragraph 4 gives us some insight into the bullying that Patricia encountered. As a result, we know that she started to hate school because the author states: "Eventually, she despised going to school." While students may be tempted to selected Letter D, the focus of this paragraph is not to describe why bullying is bad. Furthermore, the paragraph does not describe the full effects that bullying has on Patricia other than she despised going to school.

## RI.3.9. Compare And Contrast Key Points In Two Texts

1. **C.** Both passages acknowledge that cell phones may distract students from learning.

2. **D.** The author of Passage 1 thinks that students shouldn't be allowed to have phones at school at all, while the author of Passage 2 thinks students should be able to have phones at school and simply not allowed to take them out in class.

3. The author of Passage 1 thinks cell phones shouldn't be allowed in school at all, and Passage 1 only addresses bad aspects of cell phone usage. Passage 2 addresses both sides of the issue and explain some reasons that cell

phones may be good to have at school.

4. **A.** Passage 1 mentions that students may use cell phones to share answers on assignments and tests. The rest of the answer choices are mentioned in both passages, although they may not be stated in the exact words as the answer choices.

5. **1st & 4th answer choices**: (1): Students may need to contact parents in case of emergency.(4) Students and parents may need to contact one another if plans related to transportation or pick up times change.

6. **C.** The author of Passage 2 would likely say that rules about students not having cell phones in class must be enforced, or that students must be responsible enough not to use cell phones in class. However, she would argue that students do need to have cell phones at school for safety reasons and to be able to contact parents as needed (and vice versa).

7. Responses may vary. Correct answers will take a position for Passage 1 or for Passage 2 and will mention key arguments from the passage that the student found convincing.

An example of a student explanation who agrees with Passage 1 may state: I agree with Passage 1 the most. I agree with Passage 1 because cell phones do cause too much temptation. If you are too busy looking at your phone or even thinking about your phone, you are missing important information from the teacher.

An example of a student explanation who agrees with Passage 2 may state: I agree with Passage 2 the most. I agree with Passage 2 because I think students need to have them in case of an emergency. Students should be responsible enough to keep their cell phones in their backpacks during school time so that they do not get distracted.

8. **B.** Learning. Both passages mention that school is about learning and that cell phones should not interrupt the learning process.

## LANGUAGE

### L.1.1 Demonstrate Command of Grammar & Usage

1. **A.** Adjectives are used to describe or clarify

nouns by giving more information about their size, color, shape, age, material, etc.

2. **C.** The word *large* describes the noun dog, giving readers more information about its size.

3. **B.** The word *he* is a pronoun used to replace the antecedent *Mr. White.*

4. **B.** The comparative adjective *bigger* correctly completes this sentence, which compares the size of the horse to the size of the dog. -Er is added to the end of adjectives when they adjective is used to compare two nouns.

5. **D.** The plural form of the noun *bus* is the plural noun buses, so we must add an -es to the end of the word.

6. **B.** *Walked* agrees with the first-person subject I and the tense (past). This sentence is in past tense because of the word *yesterday.*

7. **A.** *Sing* correctly completes this sentence. *Sang* and *sung* are past tense, while *singing* is present tense. When combined with *will, sing* is future tense and agrees with the first-person plural subject *we.*

8. **C.** *Their* agrees with the antecedent *Michael and Jose.*

9. **B.** The speaker of the sentence wants to both go to Disney World and bring her best friends, requiring the coordinating conjunction *and.* The two sentences do not contrast, so we can't use *but* or *yet,* and *nor* is used for negative possibilities.

10. **D.** It makes sense for John to go to soccer practice *after* school. Additionally, none of the other possible options form grammatically correct sentences.

11. **B.** This sentence contains two independent clauses, so it is compound. An independent clause is a clause that can stand by itself as a sentence.

12. **C.** This sentence is complex because it contains both a dependent clause and an independent clause. A dependent clause is a clause that cannot stand by itself as a sentence.

### L.1.2 Know Capitalization, Punctuation & Spelling

1. **C.** In titles, it is necessary to capitalize the first

and last word, in addition to nouns, pronouns, verbs, and adjectives. In this title, *Lion, Witch,* and *Wardrobe* need to be capitalized. *The* must also be capitalized because it is the first word in the sentence, but any additional appearance of *the* must be lowercase. The word *and* is not capitalized because it is a conjunction.

2. **D.** When an address is written as a line of text, commas must separate the street, state, and city. Commas are not needed between words and numbers, such as the building number or the zip code.

3. **A.** Quotation marks must go only around dialogue, and the comma should be placed before the closing quotation marks.

4. **C.** This sentence correctly puts quotation marks only around dialogue. There is a comma before the closing quotation marks and between the word *said* and the additional dialogue.

5. **B.** The apostrophe s indicates possession, showing that the car belongs to the man.

6. **C.** With a plural noun, like teachers, the possessive apostrophe comes after the s instead of before. This is to indicate that the noun is both plural and possessive.

7. **A.** *Cries* is the correct spelling for the present tense form of *cry*. Cry ends with a *-y* so the *-y* is replaced by an *-i* before adding the *-es* ending.

8. **D.** The suffix -ed indicates that a verb is past tense.

9. **C.** The suffix -ing indicates that a verb is present tense.

10. **A.** The suffix -ness means "the state of" something. In this case, *happiness* is the correct word to refer to the state of being happy.

## L.2.3 Use Appropriate Language Conventions

1. **D.** Alexis was sad throughout the day because she thought everyone forgot her birthday. Before Alexis goes into the house, she thinks about how she wants to go to sleep and forget "the worst birthday ever." Based on this information, readers know that Alexis was surprised when she saw all of her friends, family, cake, and presents.

2. **B.** The characteristics listed are not common, making the starfish unique. Additionally, the phrase "unlike most animals" also hints that the correct answer is "unique."

3. **B.** The fact that the villagers had nightmares for weeks indicates that they feel terrified. *Nervous* is not strong enough to describe the way people would feel about a giant fire-breathing dragon.

4. **A.** The first blank is contrasted with what Michael Jordan could have done after not making the team (given up and decided he would never be a great basketball player). This suggests that he used not making the team as motivation. The second blank indicates that the correct word is something that can keep a person going, also showing that motivation is the correct answer.

5. **C.** The girl would feel sad about her ice cream falling on the ground. The usage of "fell" also shows that this was an accident that was not meant to happen, so readers can infer the girl felt sad about it.

6. **B.** This sentence is not a good description of the ocean. Choices A, C and D offer facts about the ocean. Choice B states an opinion that is relevant to one person.

7. **D.** This answer choice best describes a happy puppy. Choices A and C describe behaviors we would more likely see from a sad or angry puppy. Choice B doesn't necessarily indicate that the puppy is happy, so it's not a good description.

8. **A.** "You crack me up," means that someone is funny and makes you laugh.

9. **C.** Going the extra mile has nothing to do with physical distances or running. It simply means going above and beyond what is expected or required.

10. **D.** Being "under the weather" means being sick. It's also the most logical answer choice listed.

## L.3.4 Determine Meaning of Unknown Word/s in Context

1. **C.** Based on the examples of *fish, whales,* and *dolphins,* we can determine that the word **aquatic** is related to water. From the answer

ANSWER EXPLANATIONS

choices provided, water is the only option that all three examples have in common.

2. **A.** The definition of the word **sterilize** appears in the sentence when it's explained that the reason Mom sterilized the bottle was to "make sure it was clean."

3. An example of a student explanation: **Pewter** means gray. Both elephants and hippos have gray skin. The word *color* is another context clue in this sentence.

4. **C.** Because the waitress was in a bad mood, we can infer that she was not very polite to the customers.

5. **B.** This sentence indicates that the word **adept** must contrast with the word *terrible.* We know this because Jimmy was terrible at crossword puzzles, *but* his sister was very adept at them.

6. **D.** If agree means to share the same opinion about something, agreeable must mean that people are capable of/able to share an opinion on a topic.

7. Incomplete means not finished. The prefix *in* means *in, on,* or *not.* In this context, the only definition that makes sense is "not complete."

8. Preheat means to heat before, while reheat means to heat again. The prefix *pre* means *prior to, before, in advance of,* or *early,* and the prefix *re* means *back* or *again.*

9. Each of these words share the root word **sect.** The root word **sect** means cut. The prefix **bi** means twice or two. **Bisect** means to cut in two.

10. **A.** To use the word *happy* as a noun, the state of being happy, you need to use the suffix -ness. The suffix -ly transforms *happy* into an adverb. The suffixes -ing and -ed cannot be used because they would not transform *happy* into real words.

## L.3.5 Understand Word Relationships and Nuances in Meaning

1. **B.** In this sentence, the phrase *take steps* is used figuratively to mean take action or do something about it. Literal walking or running probably won't fix Chloe's relationship with her friend Naya, but taking action will.

2. **A.** This is another example of figurative language. When the sentence says that Max has *the upper hand,* it means he has the advantage over his brother. His hand being on top or being bigger is not relevant to the context of the sentence, which describes a wrestling competition. We can infer that Max has the advantage, and not the disadvantage, because he is bigger and stronger than his brother.

3. The sentence is figurative. Sarah could not literally eat a horse (and probably wouldn't want to either). This is hyperbole (exaggerated for effect), and meant to express that Sarah is extremely hungry. An example of an appropriate student explanation may state: This sentence is figurative. I know this because Sarah could not actually eat a horse. The phrase *could eat a horse* is used to show that someone is very hungry.

4. The sentence is figurative. The boy is not literally as tall as a giraffe. This is a simile meant to express that the boy is very tall. An example of an appropriate student explanation may state: This sentence is figurative. I know this because it is not possible for the boy to actually be as tall as a giraffe. The phrase as tall *as a giraffe* is used to show that someone is incredibly tall.

5. **B.** *Aggravated* is similar in meaning to *annoyed. Amused* and *joyful* are both positive words, while *annoyed* is negative. *Confused* is not relevant or close in meaning to *annoyed.*

6. **C.** *Massive* means large, so *huge* is similar in meaning. It does not refer specifically to height or length, so *short* and *long* are incorrect. *Tiny* is an antonym for *massive,* not a synonym.

7. **D.** *Fascinated* means interested or awestruck, so *bored* has the opposite meaning. *Entertained* is very close in meaning to *fascinated,* while *happy* and *scared* aren't related.

8. **B.** The word *skipped* implies that the boy was happy on his walk home, as mentioned in the sentence. *Stomped* has an angry connotation, while there's nothing in the sentence to suggest that *ran* or *tiptoed* would be a more accurate description.

9. **B.** *Furious* is a much stronger word than *mad, displeased* or *irritated.* Choice B is more powerful and implies that Anthony is more upset. An example of an appropriate student explanation may state: Furious shows that Anthony is the most upset. I know this because the words *mad, displeased,* and *irritated* do not show that Anthony is very upset.

10. **C.** Laughing is the only positive word among these choices. Frowning and smirking all have somewhat negative connotations. Staring is not related.

11. **A.** If students don't know the meaning of the word *sluggish,* it can still be inferred that *slow* is a synonym, since the turtle finished the race last. *Speedy* and *fast* wouldn't make sense in this context, and *friendly* is irrelevant to the sentence.

## L.3.6 Know Academic/ Domain-Specific Words

1. **B.** A simile is a type of figurative language that students would learn about in English/ Language Arts class.

2. **C.** The total amount when adding two or more numbers is a sum.

3. **D.** Amphibians are a class of animal that students would learn about in Science.

4. **C.** Using context clues means using the known words and phrases in a sentence to determine the meaning of the unknown word.

5. **B.** Antecedents are the nouns replaced by pronouns, and students would learn this term in English/Language Arts class.

6. **B.** Contrast means to describe the differences between two or more items.

7. **A.** The Solar System refers to the planets and moons that orbit the sun. Choice B describes the digestive system, Choice C describes the water cycle, and Choice D describes cloud types.

8. **B.** The phrase "stepping on the back of my shoes" indicates that the student is behind the writer. Additionally, the fact that the students are in line indicates "to the right of" and "next to" are most likely incorrect answers.

9. **D.** We can infer that the correct answer is "before" because the sentence includes the phrase "wake up early enough."

10. **B.** The use of the phrase "my head," in addition to knowledge about the location of an airplane, indicates that the correct answer is "above."

**ANSWER EXPLANATIONS**

# PRACTICE TEST

# SBAC ASSESSMENT

# ELA
# GRADE 3

## Practice Test One

## "My Father Meets the Cat," an excerpt from *My Father's Dragon*
### by Ruth Stiles Gannett

One cold rainy day when my father was a little boy, he met an old alley cat on his street. The cat was very drippy and uncomfortable so my father said, "Wouldn't you like to come home with me?"

This surprised the cat—she had never before met anyone who cared about old alley cats—but she said, "I'd be very much obliged if I could sit by a warm furnace, and perhaps have a saucer of milk."

My father and the cat became good friends. One day, my father and the cat went for a walk in the park.

My father said, "When I grow up I'm going to have an airplane. Wouldn't it be wonderful to fly just anywhere you might think of!"

"Would you like to fly very, very much?" asked the cat.

"I certainly would. I'd do anything if I could fly."

"Well," said the cat, "If you'd really like to fly that much, I think I know of a sort of a way you might get to fly while you're still a little boy."

"You mean you know where I could get an airplane?"

"Well, not exactly an airplane, but something even better..."

1. Who is the narrator of this story?

   **A.** A son or daughter

   **B.** A father

   **C.** An old alley cat

   **D.** Ruth Stiles Gannett

2. Based on the information in the sentence below, how would you describe the alley cat **before** she met the narrator's father?

   This surprised the cat—she had never before met anyone who cared about old alley cats—but she said, "I'd be very much obliged if I could sit by a warm furnace, and perhaps have a saucer of milk." (Paragraph 2)

   **A.** Bored

   **B.** Tired

   **C.** Lonely

   **D.** Angry

3. What is the meaning of **obliged** as it is used in the following sentence?

   "I'd be very much **obliged** if I could sit by a warm furnace, and perhaps have a saucer of milk."

   **A.** Annoyed

   **B.** Thankful

   **C.** Surprised

   **D.** Proud

4. This question has two parts. First, answer Part A. Then, answer Part B.

## Part A

What does the cat say he will do for the little boy?

   **A.** Be his friend forever.

   **B.** Take him on an exciting journey.

   **C.** Get him an airplane.

   **D.** Find a way for him to fly while he's still young.

## Part B

What sentence from the passage supports your answer to Part A?

   **A.** My father said, "When I grow up I'm going to have an airplane. Wouldn't it be wonderful to fly just anywhere you might think of!" (Paragraph 4)

   **B.** "Well," said the cat, "If you'd really like to fly that much, I think I know of a sort of a way you might get to fly while you're still a little boy." (Paragraph 7)

   **C.** "My father and the cat became good friends." (Paragraph 3)

   **D.** "You mean you know where I could get an airplane?" (Paragraph 8)

5. What is the meaning of the word **drippy** in the following sentence?

   One cold rainy day when my father was a little boy, he met an old alley cat on his street. The cat was very **drippy** and uncomfortable so my father said, "Wouldn't you like to come home with me?"

   **A.** Cold

   **B.** Sad

   **C.** Dirty

   **D.** Wet

6. The story "My Father Meets the Cat" is an excerpt from a children's novel, "My Father and the Dragon." Based on the title of the children's novel, how do you think the boy will fly? Explain your answer.

   _____

   _____

   _____

   _____

7. How does the text's image contribute to the story?

   **A.** It shows readers that the cat is cute.

   **B.** It emphasizes that the cat was sad before meeting the boy.

   **C.** It helps readers visualize the setting.

   **D.** It makes the text more interesting.

8. Reread the following paragraph.

   "My father and the cat became good friends. One day, my father and the cat went for walk in the park."

   What does this paragraph add to the passage?

   **A.** It tells readers more about the little boy.

   **B.** It explains the story's conflict.

   **C.** It helps readers understand the cat and the little boy's relationship.

   **D.** It builds suspense.

# Helping Nature to Help Us

By now, you've probably heard about global warming and climate change. These topics are a little complicated, but scientists know that our planet is getting hotter, and that's not good. Humans are the main cause of climate change.

## How Do Humans Cause Climate Change?

Some gases in Earth's atmosphere trap heat and keep it from escaping. When heat can't escape, the Earth gets hotter. These gases are called "greenhouse gases," and they include carbon dioxide and methane.

People release more carbon dioxide into the atmosphere when they cut down trees, waste electricity, burn fuels like gas, and more. The more carbon dioxide we release into the environment, the more heat gets trapped on Earth, and the hotter it gets.

## How Can I Reduce My Carbon Footprint?

Your carbon footprint is the amount of carbon dioxide that gets released because of you and your activities. If you want to help the environment, you can start by reducing your carbon footprint.

Turn off lights, the TV, and other electronics when you aren't using them. Encourage your family to walk or ride bikes instead of taking the car everywhere. Next time you go to a fast food restaurant, walk inside instead of sitting in the drive through with the car running.

## Other Ways to Help the Planet

There are other things you can do to help our planet, too. Recycle, take shorter showers, and plant a tree or a fruit/vegetable garden. When you're older, you might want to choose a "green career." These are jobs that help take care of our planet and solve problems like climate change.

9. What are 2 ways you can reduce your carbon footprint? Use evidence from the passage to support your answer.

_____

_____

_____

_____

10. What is the main idea of the passage?

   **A.** Humans are harming the planet, but there are steps we can take to help.

   **B.** The planet is in danger, but there isn't much we can do about it.

   **C.** Earth is getting hotter because of gases like carbon dioxide.

   **D.** Everyone should try to reduce their carbon footprint.

11. What does **reducing** mean as it is used in this sentence from the passage?

   If you want to help the environment, you can start by **reducing** your carbon footprint.

   **A.** Increasing, or making larger

   **B.** Getting rid of

   **C.** Decreasing, or making smaller

   **D.** Learning about

12. Which information can be found under the heading **How Do Humans Cause Climate Change?**

   **A.** The opinions of famous scientists

   **B.** Information about greenhouse gases

   **C.** Information about how people can stop causing climate change

   **D.** The definition of climate change

13. This question has two parts. First, answer Part A. Then, answer Part B.

## Part A

Based on the information in the passage, with which statement would the author most likely agree?

   **A.** Humans aren't to blame for climate change or global warming.

   **B.** If we want to save our planet, we should never ride in cars.

   **C.** People can take small steps, like planting a tree, to help the planet.

   **D.** There's nothing we can do to stop the planet from getting warmer.

## Part B

Which piece of evidence from the passage supports your answer in Part A?

   **A.** "Your carbon footprint is the amount of carbon dioxide that gets released because of you and your activities." (Paragraph 4)

   **B.** "People release more carbon dioxide into the atmosphere when they cut down trees, waste electricity, burn fuels like gas, and more." (Paragraph 3)

   **C.** "By now, you've probably heard about global warming and climate change. These topics are a little complicated, but scientists know that our planet is getting hotter, and that's not good." (Paragraph 1)

   **D.** "There are other things you can do to help our planet, too. Recycle, take shorter showers, and plant a tree or a fruit/vegetable garden." (Paragraph 6)

14. Which type of organization does the author use in this passage? Select **ALL** correct answers.
    - ☐ Cause and effect
    - ☐ Problem and solution
    - ☐ Chronological order
    - ☐ Sequencing

15. This question has two parts. First, answer Part A. Then, answer Part B.

## Part A

How do greenhouse gases cause global warming?

   **A.** They trap heat, which causes the Earth to get hotter.
   **B.** They release more heat into the atmosphere.
   **C.** They pollute the planet.
   **D.** They kill trees and dry up oceans, which increases heat.

## Part B

Which sentence in the passage supports your answer in Part A?

   **A.** "People release more carbon dioxide into the atmosphere when they cut down trees, waste electricity, burn fuels like gas, and more." (Paragraph 3)
   **B.** "Your carbon footprint is the amount of carbon dioxide that gets released because of you and your activities." (Paragraph 4)
   **C.** "The more carbon dioxide we release into the environment, the more heat gets trapped on Earth, and the hotter it gets." (Paragraph 3)
   **D.** "When you're older, you might want to choose a "green career." These are jobs that help take care of our planet and solve problems like climate change." (Paragraph 6)

16. According to the information in the passage, what are some ways you can help the environment (other than reducing your carbon footprint)? Check **ALL** correct answers.
    - ☐ Plant a garden
    - ☐ Pick up trash on the ground
    - ☐ Recycle
    - ☐ Take shorter showers
    - ☐ Turn the water off when brushing your teeth
    - ☐ Plant a tree
    - ☐ Choose a "green" career

17. Justin is writing a report for his teacher about animal adaptations. He wants to revise his report to make sure it has enough details. Read this portion of the report and complete the task that follows.

One type of adaptation that animals have is defense. Defense is how animals protect themselves from predators. <u>Animals can have many different physical attributes that can help protect them from other animals.</u> Some animals have to defend themselves from bigger animals that are searching for food. Other animals might protect themselves by hiding from potential predators. In addition, animals may use their adaptations to warn other animals to stay away.

**My Notes on Animal Adaptations:**
- Adaptations help an animal survive in its natural habitat
- Predators hunt other animals for food
- Animals that are taken and eaten by other animals are prey
- Tigers have striped fur to blend in with their environment
- The bright colors of the poison dart frog warn other animals that it is not safe to eat
- Fur helps animals stay warm in cold climates

Choose the two sentences from Justin's notes that add more facts to the information given in the underlined sentence.

- ☐ Adaptations help an animal survive in its natural habitat.
- ☐ Predators hunt other animals for food.
- ☐ Animals that are taken and eaten by other animals are prey.
- ☐ Tigers have striped fur to blend in with their environment.
- ☐ The bright colors of the poison dart frog warn other animals that it is not safe to eat.
- ☐ Fur helps animals stay warm in cold climates.

18. Nevaeh is writing an opinion essay about assigning homework to students in elementary school. Read the draft of her essay and complete the task that follows.

Most people think that homework helps students do better in school. However, some people think that students in elementary school should not have homework. Some students have parents that work at night and cannot help children with homework. Some people also say that homework can cause unnecessary stress and anxiety on students. Other people think that homework might prevent students from participating in after school activities, playing sports, or spending time with family and friends. Students work hard enough in school during the day.

The beginning of Nevaeh's essay does not state her opinion. Write an opening paragraph that states the opinion and explains what the topic is about.

_____

_____

_____

_____

_____

_____

_____

19. Aaron is writing a story about getting a new dog. He wants to revise his story to use more descriptive words. Read the draft and complete the task that follows.

"Woof, woof!" When we stepped into the shelter, all I could hear was dogs barking. It felt like all the dogs were staring at us, saying "Pick me! Pick me!"
My mom wanted to make sure that we picked out a dog that would be good with kids. She also wanted a dog that had a lot of energy because our family enjoyed going on day trips, hiking, biking, and going to the park.
"How about this one, Mom?" I asked, as I approached a dog who was wagging his tail and standing up against the gate. Mom looked at the dog.
Mom asked the man at the shelter if we could see Gus, which was the dog's name. The man opened the gate and Gus immediately ran over to me and jumped on me, kissing my face.
Mom smiled and laughed.

Select **two** of the choices that have the **best** descriptive sentences to replace
<u>Mom looked at the dog</u> and <u>Mom smiled and laughed</u>.

☐ Mom looked thoughtfully at the dog. / Mom smiled and started laughing.

☐ Mom gave the dog a soft look that seemed to say, "Would you like to come home with us?" / As Mom smiled and chuckled to herself, she said "Well, I guess this one is a keeper, huh? What do you think Gus? Would you like to come home with us?"

☐ Mom stared at the dog./Mom burst out laughing.

☐ Mom approached the dog in his gate and gazed at him thoughtfully. / I couldn't stop laughing as Gus licked my face. I looked over at Mom, and she was laughing, too. As Mom and I looked at each other and then at Gus, we knew Gus was perfect.

☐ Mom glanced at the dog. / Mom looked at Gus kissing my face and laughed.

☐ Mom made eye contact with Gus as he wagged his tail. / Mom smiled a soft smile and laughed.

20. Choose the sentence that contains a spelling error.

    **A.** The girl was sitting underneath the tree to enjoy the shade from the sun.

    **B.** The baby crys when he is hungry or tired.

    **C.** We had to clean the house because company was coming over.

    **D.** I have to walk the dog when I return home from the movies.

21. Choose the two sentences that have mistakes in punctuation.

    ☐ Shawn and I collected seashells as we walked on the beach.

    ☐ "Look at this smooth and shiny shell! I shouted to Shawn.

    ☐ Shawn and I had fun building a huge sandcastle.

    ☐ We had to build the sandcastle again because the waves destroyed it.

    ☐ The supplies we will need to make the sandcastle are, shells: rocks: sand: and buckets.

    ☐ "This is the best day I've ever had at the beach!" Shawn exclaimed.

**Please note that this section of the test contains 'Listening Items' for question numbers 22-27.**

**Directions: This is an Audio Presentation. Students should listen to another person reading the presentation "Hummingbird", then answer the questions below.**

## Hummingbirds

If you've ever been close to a hummingbird, you've probably heard the buzzing noise they make when they fly. Hummingbirds make this noise because of how quickly they can flap their wings. They can beat their wings as many as 80 times in a single second! This gives them the ability to hover in the air, like a helicopter. Hummingbirds are also the only bird that flies backwards.

Moving so fast requires a lot of energy. This means that hummingbirds need to eat more than you would expect for such a small bird. Their favorite food is nectar, a sweet liquid that can be found inside flowers. Hummingbirds have to visit hundreds of flowers to get enough nectar each day. Every day, they drink more than their body weight in nectar.

It looks like hummingbirds use their long beaks like straws, but they really use their tongues to drink nectar. They lap up nectar from flowers the same way your dog or cat might lap up water from a bowl.

Flowers feed hummingbirds and help them gain energy, but hummingbirds help flowers too. When hummingbirds drink nectar, they get pollen from the flowers on their heads and beaks. Pollen is what helps flowers make seeds.

As the hummingbirds fly to more flowers to drink more nectar, they also spread pollen and help flowers make more seeds. Then more flowers grow, and the hummingbird has even more nectar to drink!

**Now answer the questions below. Base your answers on the presentation you have just heard.**

22. According to the presentation **"Hummingbird"**, why do hummingbirds require so much energy?
    **A.** They need energy to fly for long distances.
    **B.** They are large birds who need plenty of energy.
    **C.** They are small birds who need enough energy to fight off larger predators.
    **D.** They need energy because they move so quickly.

23. Which statement BEST describes the relationship between hummingbirds and flowers?
    A. Flowers help hummingbirds by giving them food and energy.
    B. Hummingbirds help flowers by spreading their seeds.
    C. Hummingbirds and flowers have a mutually helpful relationship, that is they both help each other
    D. Hummingbirds eat the nectar from flowers.

**Directions: This is an Audio Presentation. Students should listen to another person reading the presentation "Honey Badgers", then answer the questions below.**

## Honey Badgers

Honey badgers aren't very big, but they sure are tough. They're only a couple feet long and weigh just over 20 pounds, but they've been known to chase away lions. After they chase away the lions, they take the food the lions have hunted and eat it for themselves instead.

How can such a tiny animal be so tough? The honey badger is equipped with helpful weapons. For example, honey badgers have extremely thick skin. Arrows, bites from other animals, and even small bullets can't pierce the honey badgers' tough skin. Honey badger's teeth are strong too. A honey badger can bite through a turtle shell.

Honey badgers also have long, sharp claws. The claws are great for fighting off predators, but they're also useful for digging. Honey badgers can dig a nine-foot tunnel in just 10 minutes. They use this ability to construct their homes, which are small tunnels in the ground. If any predator approaches the honey badger's home, even a cow or a horse, the honey badgers will attack fiercely to defend their territory.

If honey badgers are so ferocious, why do they have such a "sweet" name? Well, honey badgers love to eat honey. Because their skin is so tough, they can invade beehives without being injured with bee stings. Beekeepers in Africa have to use electric fences to keep honey badgers from eating all of the honey their bees produce.

24. According to the presentation **"Honey Badgers"**, which of the following is NOT a helpful weapon for honey badgers?
    **A.** Strong teeth
    **B.** Black eyes
    **C.** Sharp claws
    **D.** Tough skin

25. What is the main idea of the passage **"Honey Badgers"**?
    **A.** Honey badgers are both sweet and vicious.
    **B.** Honey badgers are much tougher than they look.
    **C.** Honey badgers are dangerous for bees.
    **D.** Honey badgers can scare off lions.

26. With which statement would the author of the passage **"Honey Badgers"** most likely agree?

    A. Honey badgers can successfully fight or scare off much bigger predators.

    B. Honey badgers should have a different name, because they aren't sweet like their name suggests.

    C. Beekeepers should not build electric fences to keep out honey badgers as it may harm the badgers.

    D. Honey badgers are at a disadvantage with other predators because of their small size.

27. What is one way that hummingbirds and honey badgers are similar?

    A. They both have special weapons to fight off predators.

    B. They both like to eat honey.

    C. They both make buzzing noises, although for different reasons.

    D. Their small sizes can be misleading: Honey badgers are tough, and hummingbirds eat a lot.

28. Miranda is writing a research report about the Cheyenne Native Americans. Read the sentences from her report and the directions that follow.

    The Cheyenne Native Americans lived in the Great Plains region of the United States. The Cheyenne relied on the buffalo for food, clothing, and shelter. Therefore, the Cheyenne had to frequently move in order to follow the buffalo herds. Tipis were a very useful shelter for this purpose.

    Choose two of the sources that would most likely give Miranda more information about the ideas she has written.

    ☐ www.bigorrin.org/cheyenne_kids.htm, a website that gives facts about the Cheyenne

    ☐ *Atlas of Indian Nations*, a book that tells the history and culture of Native Americans

    ☐ *The Life of Pocahontas*, a biography

    ☐ *The Cheyenne*, a book that includes information about Cheyenne homes, food, clothing, crafts, and life today

    ☐ www.native-languages.org, a website devoted to preserving and promoting American Indian languages

    ☐ *The Indian in the Cupboard*, a fantasy novel about a plastic figurine that comes to life

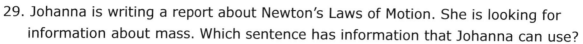

29. Johanna is writing a report about Newton's Laws of Motion. She is looking for information about mass. Which sentence has information that Johanna can use?

    **A.** It takes more force to lift a box of books than it does to lift one book.

    **B.** Matter is anything that takes up space and has mass.

    **C.** An object at rest stays at rest and an object in motion stays in motion unless acted upon by an outside force.

    **D.** Mass is the amount of matter an object has, not how much weight an object has.

30. Nico is writing a research report about Martin Luther King, Jr. He took notes and thought of three main ideas for his report. Select the box to show the main idea that each note best supports.

| | **Main Idea A:** Martin Luther King, Jr. led non-violent protests to fight for the civil rights of all people, including African Americans. | **Main Idea B:** Martin Luther King, Jr. helped to pave the way for many of the civil rights we all share today. | **Main Idea C:** Martin Luther King, Jr.'s childhood set the foundation for the inspiring work he would do as an adult. |
|---|---|---|---|
| **Note 1:** Martin Luther King, Jr. was born in Atlanta, Georgia on January 15, 1929. | ☐ | ☐ | ☐ |
| **Note 2:** After Martin Luther King, Jr. gave his "I Have A Dream Speech", segregation in public schools was eliminated. | ☐ | ☐ | ☐ |
| **Note 3:** Martin Luther King, Jr. organized the Montgomery Bus Boycott after Rosa Parks was arrested for refusing to give up her bus seat to a white man. | ☐ | ☐ | ☐ |
| **Note 4:** Martin Luther King, Jr. graduated high school 2 years early and started college at age 14. | ☐ | ☐ | ☐ |

31. Gabriel is writing a research report about the different parts of a map. He wrote an opinion in the report. Read the sentences from Gabriel's report and the directions that follow.

**Parts of a Map**

A map has many different parts. In order to read a map, you need to know how to use the different parts of the map. Some parts of a map might be: a map key, symbols, a compass, and a map scale. Using a compass to find the locations of different places can be confusing.

Gabriel found another source about the parts of a map. Which sentence best supports Gabriel's opinion?

    **A.** For example, a compass can include cardinal directions such as North, South, East, and West.

    **B.** For example, a compass can include intermediate directions such as: Northwest, Northeast, Southeast, and Southwest.

    **C.** For example, Florida is located Southeast of Nebraska.

    **D.** For example, sometimes you need to use a compass with cardinal directions and intermediate directions at the same time to find where a place is located.

32. Muhammad is writing a report about penguins. Read the sentences from the source and the directions that follow.

Emperor penguins live in cold climates. Most Emperor penguins will spend their entire lives on the Antarctic ice and the surrounding waters. Penguins have a thick layer of fat that protects them when they swim in the icy, cold waters. Their outer feathers are also covered with a special oil that helps to keep the penguins dry.

The parts of Muhammad's report are listed below. Where in the report should Muhammad place the information from this source?

    **A.** Penguin Babies

    **B.** How Penguins Catch Food

    **C.** Penguin Adaptations

    **D.** How Penguins Defend Themselves

33. Charlie wrote an essay about staying healthy. Read the sentences from Charlie's essay and the directions that follow.

There are lots of things that kids can do to stay healthy. First, kids should make sure they eat a healthy breakfast that includes protein. Kids should also pack a healthy snack for school. For example, fruit and vegetables are good choices for a school snack. It is also important for kids to exercise. Kids should spend more time being active than watching television and playing video games.

Which of the following statements would Charlie most likely agree?
   **A.** Kids should never eat dessert.
   **B.** Playing tag is one way to exercise.
   **C.** Parents should not buy televisions for kids.
   **D.** It is more important to be healthy than it is to do good in school.

# ANSWER EXPLANATIONS

## SBAC ELA Practice Test One
## Session 1
## Answer Explanations

1. **A.** The narrator of this story is a son or daughter. Although the story focuses on the father, it his son or daughter who is telling readers about something that happened to the father as a young boy. **(Standard: RL.2.6)**

2. **C.** The cat seems lonely based on the provided information. The cat is surprised by the boy's kindness because "she had never before met anyone who cared about old alley cats." Readers can infer that if the cat has never met anyone who cared about her, then she has been very lonely. **(Standard: RL.1.3)**

3. **B.** The cat would be thankful to have something to drink and a warm place to rest, especially because no one has showed her kindness in the past. **(Standard: RL.2.4)**

4. Part A- **D.** The cat says he might know a way for the child to fly while he's still a little boy.

Part B- **B.** This quote indicates that the cat will help the boy fly while he's still young. The rest of the text makes it clear that while she will help the boy fly, it won't be with an airplane. **(Standard: RL.1.1)**

5. **D.** Wet. The passage explains that it is raining when the boy finds the cat, so we can infer that "drippy" is referring to the cat being wet, with rain dripping from its fur. **(Standard: RL.2.4)**

6. The title of the children's novel is *My Father and the Dragon*. The passage makes it clear that the boy won't fly on an airplane, but he will fly using "something even better." Based on this title, we can infer that the "something even better" is a dragon. **(Standard: RL.1.1)**

7. **B.** The image emphasizes that the cat was sad and lonely prior to meeting the boy. It helps readers visualize how the cat looked when the boy ran into him and understand why the boy felt compelled to treat the cat so kindly. **(Standard: RL.3.7)**

8. **C.** Paragraph 3 gives readers information about the cat and the boy's relationship, explaining that they have developed a close friendship. **(Standard: RL.2.5)**

9. **Answers may vary slightly.** Appropriate answers will include any 2 of the following examples: walking inside instead of waiting in the drive through, walking or biking instead of riding in a car, turn off the lights when you aren't using them, and unplugging electronics. **(Standard: RI.1.1)**

10. **A.** This answer adequately summarizes the main idea of the passage. Choice B is untrue, and choices C and D only cover specific parts of the passage, rather than the main idea of the passage as a whole. The passage is about the damage humans are doing to the planet, in addition to the steps we can take to help. **(Standard: RI.1.2)**

11. **C.** Students can help the planet by making their carbon footprint smaller. Students should infer that they can't get rid of their carbon footprint altogether, because they will sometimes use electricity, drive or ride in cars, etc. **(Standard: RI.2.4)**

12. **B.** Information about greenhouse gases can be found under the heading "How Do Humans Cause Climate Change?" To answer the questions, students must be able to locate the appropriate heading and skim the information presented. **(Standard: RI.2.5)**

13. Part A- **C.** The author would agree with the statement that people can take small steps, like planting a tree, to help the planet. Other statements are too extreme, like we should "never" ride in cars or there's nothing people can do to help the planet

Part B- **D.** This quote from the passage shows the author's belief that there are things people can do to help the planet, such as planting trees. **(Standard: RI.2.6)**

14. **1st and 2nd answer choices.** The start of the passage is organized by the author describing the cause and effect of human behavior on the planet. The second half of the passage is organized by introducing solutions for the problem (global warming and climate change). Chronological order and sequencing are not used to organize the passage. **(Standard: RI.1.3)**

15. Part A- **A.** Greenhouse gases trap heat. When heat can't escape, the planet gets hotter.

Part B- **C.** This quote directly explains how greenhouse gases heat Earth and cause global warming. **(Standard: RI.1.1)**

16. **1st, 3rd, 4th, 6th and 7th Choices.** Students should select plant a garden, recycle, take shorter showers, plant a tree, and choose a "green" career. While other answer choices could possibly help the environment, they are not specifically mentioned in the passage. **(Standard: RI.1.1, RI.1.3)**

17. **4th and 5th Choices.**

Students should select the 4th and 5th answer

choices: Tigers have striped fur to blend with their environment and The bright colors of the poison dart frog warn other animals that it is not safe to eat.

These answer choices provide further detail to the underlined sentence: Animals can have many different physical attributes that can help protect them from other animals.

While the remaining answer choices are related to animal adaptations, they are NOT related to the physical attributes that provide protection. **(Standard: 3.W.2.b)**

18. **Answers may vary.** An exemplar response worth 2 points will:

- introduce an opinion that adequately reflects the details in the paragraph

- provides sufficient information to put the opinion about the topic into context

- does more than list points/reasons to support opinion

- provides an adequate connection to the body paragraph

An example of an exemplar response is: Some people argue that students need to have homework every night, while others believe students shouldn't have any homework. I believe that students should not have homework. It is true that homework can review important concepts taught in school, but I think there are many more benefits to not having homework.

A response worth 1 point will:

- provides an opinion that partially reflects the details in the paragraph

- provides partial or general information to put the opinion about the topic in context

- may just list ideas

- provides limited connection to the body paragraph

An example of a response worth 1 point is: I do not think students should have homework anymore. Now I will tell you why I think this.

A response worth 0 points will:

- provide no opinion or no appropriate opinion, or simply restates the reasons about why students shouldn't have homework

- provides no relevant or no information to put the opinion in context

- provides a weak, if any, connection to the body paragraph

An example of a response worth 0 points is: I think students should have homework every night. **(Standard: 3.W.1.a)**

19. **2nd and 4th Choices.** Mom gave the dog a soft look that seemed to say, "Would you like to come home with us?" / As Mom smiled and chuckled to herself, she said "Well, I guess this one is a keeper, huh? What do you think Gus? Would you like to come home with us?" and Mom approached the dog in his gate and gazed at him thoughtfully. / I couldn't stop laughing as Gus licked my face. I looked over at Mom, and she was laughing, too. As Mom and I looked at each other and then at Gus, we knew Gus was perfect.

These answer choices provide better descriptions of the underlined sentences: Mom looked at the dog and Mom smiled and laughed. These answer choices make the reader feel as though they are inside the story, including thoughts, feelings, and actions while also including appropriate dialogue. **(Standard: 3.W.3.b)**

20. **B.** Crys is spelled incorrectly. To show the present tense of cry, you need to drop the -y and add -ies to the ending to make cries. **(Standard: 3.L.2)**

21. **2nd and 5th Choices.** The 2nd answer choice incorrectly uses quotation marks. The sentence should read: "Look at this smooth and shiny shell!" I shouted to Shawn. The 5th answer choices incorrectly uses a colon and commas in a series. The sentence should read: The supplies we will need to make the sandcastle are: shells, rocks, sand, and buckets. **(Standard: 3.L.2)**

22. **D.** Hummingbirds need energy because they move so quickly. The passage explains that although hummingbirds are small, they must eat a lot to help them maintain the energy to beat their wings so quickly. Hummingbirds beat their wings as many as 80 times in a single second. **(Standard: RI.1.1)**

23. **C.** Hummingbirds and flowers have a mutually helpful relationship. The flowers feed and provide energy to the hummingbirds, and the hummingbirds help pollinate the flowers. **(Standard: RI.1.3)**

24. **B.** The passage does not mention the honey badgers having black eyes. It does, however, specify that honey badgers use their strong teeth, sharp claws, and tough skin to protect themselves and fight predators. **(Standard: RI.1.1)**

25. **B.** The main idea of this passage is that honey badgers are much tougher than they look. The passage starts off by mentioning that honey badgers are relatively small, but the rest of the

passage focuses on all the way honey badgers are more tough and ferocious than one would expect. **(Standard: RI.1.2)**

26. **A.** The author would agree that honey badgers can fight off much bigger predators. Although they're small, their size is not a disadvantage thanks to their arsenal of weapons and their fierce personalities. The quote about the badgers defending their homes against even horses and cows, who are much bigger than the honey badger, supports this point. **(Standard: RI.2.6)**

27. **D.** The small size of both the honey badger and the hummingbird can be misleading. Hummingbirds eat much more food than one would expect, and honey badgers are far more fierce and intimidating than one would think. **(Standard: RI.3.9)**

28. **1st and 4th Choices.** These 2 choices will provide additional information about the Cheyenne Native Americans. *The Atlas of Indian Nations* would not be one of the most useful sources because it tells about all Native Americans. *The Life of Pocahontas* is not relevant because it is a biography about one person. The website www.native-languages.org is not appropriate because it describes Native American languages. *The Indian in the Cupboard* is not appropriate because it is a fiction novel. **(Standard: 3.W.8)**

29. **D** Letter *D* has information that Johanna can use because it is directly related to mass. While Letter *B* mentions mass, it is as part of the definition of matter and therefore not as relevant.

Letters *A* and *C* are more specific to Newton's Laws of Motion rather than mass. **(Standard: 3.RI.1)**

30. Note 1 supports Main Idea C because it relates to Martin Luther King, Jr.'s childhood. Note 2 supports Main Idea B because it is related to the effects that Martin Luther King, Jr.'s work has had on civil rights progress and achievements. Note 3 supports Main Idea A because it is an example of a non-violent protest led by Martin Luther King, Jr. Note 4 supports Main Idea C because it relates to Martin Luther King Jr.'s childhood.

31. **D.** Gabriel's opinion is that using a compass to find locations can be confusing. Letter D supports Gabriel's opinion because it describes how you sometimes have to use cardinal directions and intermediate directions at the same time to find a location on a map. **(Standard: 3.W.1.b, 3.RI.1)**

32. **C.** The information from the source describes different adaptations that penguins have allowing them to survive in the arctic climate. **(Standard: 3.W.8)**

33. **B.** Charlie's opinion is that there are lots of things kids can do to stay healthy. Letter B supports his opinion because it is an example of how kids can stay healthy.

There is not enough information in the paragraph to support that Charlie would agree that children should never eat dessert, that parents should not buy televisions for kids, or that it is more important to be healthy than to do well in school. **(Standard: 3.RI.73.RI.6)**

# PERFORMANCE TASK

# Performance Task

Your class has been learning about famous inventors. Your teacher has asked each student to learn about a famous inventor. You think that cell phones are interesting, and you want to learn more about who invented them. You have found two sources about the invention of cell phones.

After you have reviewed these sources, you will answer some questions about them. Briefly scan these sources and the three questions that follow. Then, go back and reread the sources carefully so you will have the information you need to answer the questions and complete your research. You may use scratch paper to take notes.

In Part 2, you will write an informational article using information you have read.

## Directions for Beginning
You will now review 2 sources. You can review either source as often as you like.

## Research Questions

After reviewing the research questions, use the rest of the time in Part 1 to answer three questions about them. Your answers to these questions will be scored. Also, your answers will help you think about the information you have read and viewed, which should help you write your informational article.

You may refer back to your scratch paper to review your notes when you think it would be helpful. Answer the questions in the spaces below the items. Your scratch paper will be available to you in Part 1 and Part 2 of the Performance Task.

## Part 1

### Sources for Performance Task:

**Source #1:** You have found a source describing the history of the mobile phone.

### Transformation of the Mobile Phone

Did you know that the first mobile phone was almost as long as your arm? Now, cell phones are small enough to fit in your pocket. However, this transformation didn't happen overnight. Mobile phones have been undergoing changes since they first existed as car phones in the late 1940's.

In the late 1940's, car phones allowed people to make and receive phone calls while driving in cars. The engineers of Bell Labs introduced this limited system to the United States. Unfortunately, the coverage area was very small, and technology didn't allow for a high volume of mobile traffic at that time.

In 1968, the Federal Communications Commission (FCC) stated that if technology could support better mobile service, they would allow greater frequencies for communication to exist. In other words, the FCC would open the airwaves to allow for more mobile conversations to occur.

Dr. Martin Cooper, who worked for Motorola at the time, made the first phone call on a portable cell phone in 1973. Cooper is credited with inventing the first handheld mobile phone. This mobile phone only allowed for 30 minutes of conversation and required 10 hours to charge.

Overtime, cell phones became smaller and served numerous purposes. In 1997, cellphones changed drastically with the invention of the internet. The Synergy by Philips Consumer Communications introduced the cell phone that contains many of the popular features known today. For example, the cell phone had a touch screen and used wireless connection to gain access to e-mail and the internet. As text messaging became more popular in 2002, the T-Mobile introduced the Sidekick. This phone had a screen that flipped out allow full keyboard access, making text messaging quicker and more efficient. The Sidekick also had games, apps, and a camera. In 2007, Apple introduced the first iPhone. The smart phone contains a touch screen, camera, music player, internet access, and more apps than can be counted.

What started as a simple way for mobile communication has now revolutionized how people communicate and how people access technology. Cell phones were originally created so that people could communicate no matter where they were located. Now, people basically carry a computer in their back pocket or purse. What was once the size of a brick can now fit in the palm of your hand, serving much more than just the purpose of long-distance communications.

**Sources Used:**

New Writing, Technogensis CS 2367 .04 2015, Cell phones as an extension of humans. Retrieved from: https://newwritingtechnogenesis.wordpress.com/2015/05/01/cellphones-as-an-extension-of-humans/

ThoughtCo. The history of cellular phones. Retrieved from: https://www.thoughtco.com/history-of-cellular-phones-4072557

**Source #2:** You have found a source about the inventor of cell phones.

## Dr. Martin Cooper, Making Mobile Communication Possible

The concept of cellular communication was first introduced by AT & T. Bell Labs invented a system that would allow for calls to be made from one cell to another. However, this system was restricted to automobile use only. Dr. Martin Cooper and his fellow colleagues of Motorola wanted to design a system that was more portable and more widespread.

Dr. Martin Cooper and Motorola constructed a prototype over the course of three months. In April of 1973, Cooper made the first phone call using a portable handheld device in New York City. The prototype, named the Motorola Dyna-Tac, was about 11 inches high, about 4 inches thick, and weighed almost 3 pounds. The prototype allowed for 30 minutes of talk time and required 10 hours to recharge. As a prototype, the product was not yet available for commercial sale.

The Motorola Dyna-Tac 800X was first released 10 years later in 1983. When Dr. Cooper's prototype was available for commercial sale, it cost approximately $4,000. The Motorola Dyna-Tac 800X still allowed for 30 minutes of conversation and could store up to 30 phone numbers. It wasn't until the 1990s that phones were more affordable and user friendly.

Through the 1990s and 2000s, cell phones transformed rapidly. Devices that were once used solely for mobile communication became technological power houses. Through the years, the cell phone had improvements such as: smaller size, longer battery life, touch screens, internet access, faster processing speed, and access to countless apps.

When Dr. Martin Cooper invented the first cell phone in 1973, he could have never imagined the technological advances that would be made in his lifetime. Cooper continues to work in the cell phone industry as the founder of ArrayComm, a company striving to improve wireless communication. Cooper and his wife even invented the Jitterbug, a simple smart phone made specifically for senior citizens. No one knows what the cell phone will look like 10 years from now, but we do know what it looked like at the very beginning. With the technological improvements that are made on a day-to-day basis, the possibilities for future mobile devices are endless!

**Sources Used:**

CNN. (2010). Inventor of cell phone: We knew someday everybody would have one. Retrieved from: http://www.cnn.com/2010/TECH/mobile/07/09/cooper.cell.phone.inventor/index.html

Know Your Mobile. (2017, March 6). The history of mobile phones from 1973 to 2008: the handsets that made it all happen. Retrieved from: http://www.knowyourmobile.com/nokia/nokia-3310/19848/history-mobile-phones-1973-2008-handsets-made-it-all-happen

Tech-Faq. Who invented the cell phone? Retrieved from: http://www.tech-faq.com/who-invented-the-cell-phone.html

1. Which source **most likely** has the most useful information about how cell phones have changed over time? Explain why this source **most likely** has the most useful information about how cell phones have changed over time. Support your explanation with **two** details from the source.

_____

_____

_____

_____

_____

_____

_____

2. Explain why the cell phone was not as user friendly when it was first invented. Give **two** reasons from Source #1 and **one** reason from Source #2. For each reason, include the source title or number.

_____

_____

_____

_____

_____

_____

_____

_____

_____

_____

3. Select the boxes to match each source with the idea or ideas that it supports. Some ideas may have **more than one** source selected.

| | Source #1: Transformation of the Mobile Phone | Source #2: Dr. Martin Cooper, Making Mobile Communication Possible |
|---|---|---|
| Apple introduced the first iPhone in 2007. | ☐ | ☐ |
| Dr. Martin Cooper and his wife invented the Jitterbug. | ☐ | ☐ |
| Today's phones have access to the internet, many apps, and touch screens. | ☐ | ☐ |
| Dr. Martin Cooper made the first phone call on a handheld device in 1973. | ☐ | ☐ |

**Student Directions**

**Famous Inventor Performance Task**

**Part 2**

You will review your notes and sources, and plan, draft, revise, and edit your writing. You may use your notes and go back to the sources. Now read your assignment and the information about how your writing will be scored, then begin your work.

**Your Assignment:**

Your class will be having an Invention Day. Each student will dress up as the famous inventor he/she researched and present a project explaining what you learned about the famous inventor. You decide to write an informational article about the inventor of cell phones. Your article will be read by other teachers, students, and parents.

Using more than one source, develop a main idea about the man who invented cell phones. Choose the most important information from the sources to support your main idea. Then, write an informational article that is several paragraphs long. Clearly organize your article and support your main idea with details from the sources. Use your own words except when quoting directly from the sources. Be sure to give the source title or number when using details from the sources.

**REMEMBER: A well-written informational article**

- has a clear main idea.
- is well-organized and stays on topic.
- has an introduction and conclusion.
- uses transitions.
- uses details from the sources to support your main idea.
- puts the information from the sources in your own words, except when using direct quotations from the sources.
- gives the title or number of the source for the details or facts you included.
- develops ideas clearly.
- uses clear language.
- follows rules of writing (spelling, punctuation, and grammar.)

_____

_____

_____

_____

_____

_____

_____

_____

_____

_____

_____

_____

_____

_____

_____

_____

_____

# PERFORMANCE TASK ANSWER EXPLANATIONS

## SBAC ELA Performance Task One Answer Explanations

1. **See detailed explanation**.

Source #1: Transformation of the Mobile Phone

- Cell phones were once as long as your arm. Now they can fit in your back pocket.
- 1st handheld device allowed 30 minutes of conversation and took 10 hours to charge.
- Cell phones have become smaller overtime and serve multiple purposes.
- Cell phones changed drastically with the invention of the internet in 1997.
- T-Mobile introduced the Side Kick when text messaging became more popular.

A response worth 2 points is: evidence based, correctly identifies the most useful source, includes 2 details from that source, and explains why each detail supports the idea that it is the most useful source.

An example of an exemplar response worth 2 points is: Source #1 has the most useful information about the changes cell phones have undergone over time. This source is the most useful because it describes the changes made to cell phones since they were first invented in the 1940's. For example, Source #1 says that the first cell phone was as long as a person's arm, but now they can fit in your pocket. This is important because it explains how the size of cell phones has changed over time. Source #1 also says that in 2002, the T-Mobile phone came with a Side Kick, which was a flip keyboard. This is important because it shows how the cell phone changed to make text messaging easier for people.

A response worth 1 point is: evidence based, correctly identifies the most useful source, includes 1 detail from that source, and explains why the detail supports the idea that it is the most useful source; OR

is evidence based, correctly identifies the most useful source, and includes 2 details from that source, but does not explain why each detail supports the idea that it is from the most useful source; OR

is evidence based, does not identify a source or does not identify correctly identify the most useful source, includes 2 details from the correct source, and explains why each detail supports the idea that it is from the most useful source.

An example of a response worth 1 point is: Source #1 has the most useful information about the changes cell phones have undergone over time. This source is the most useful because it describes the changes made to cell phones since they were first invented in the 1940's. For example, Source #1 says that the first cell phone was as long as a person's arm, but now they can fit in your pocket. Source #1 also says that in 2002, the T-Mobile phone came with a Side Kick, which was a flip keyboard.

A response worth 0 points is: incorrect, irrelevant, insufficient, and blank. An example of a response worth 0 points is: Source #2 has the most useful information about the changes cell phones have undergone over time. **(3.W.8, 3.RI.9)**

2. **See detailed explanation**.

Source #1: Transformation of the Mobile Phone
- The first cell phones were only for automobiles.
- First cell phones were as long as an arm.
- Cover was small and technology didn't allow for a high volume of mobile traffic.
- The first mobile phone only allowed 30 minutes of conversation.
- The first mobile phone took 10 hours to charge.

Source #2: Dr. Martin Cooper, Making Mobile Communication Possible
- Dr. Cooper's cell phone prototype was 11 inches high, 4 inches think, and weight about 3 pounds
- Dr. Cooper's cell phone prototype only allowed for 30 minutes of talk time.
- Dr. Cooper's cell phone prototype took 10 hours to charge.
- When Dr. Cooper's cell phone was available for commercial sale, it cost $4,000.

A response worth 2 points is: evidence based, correctly identifies the most useful source, includes 2 details from that source, and explains why each detail supports the idea that it is the most useful source.

An exemplar example of a response worth 2 points is: The cell phone was not as user friendly as it is now. When it was first invented, it was hard for people to get a hold of and it was hard for people to use. Source #1 says that the first cell phone was only for automobiles. This is important because not everyone was able to afford a car. This is also important because mobile conversations couldn't be had unless they were in the car. Source #1 also says that the first cell phone took 10 hours to charge. This is important because the phone would have to be on charge for more hours than it could be used for. This would make it very difficult to use the phone whenever you wanted to. Source #2 says that the first cell phone also cost about $4,000. This is important because only the very rich people could afford cell phones. This also means that at first, most people couldn't even purchase a cell phone.

A response worth 1 point is: evidence based, provides 2 pieces of evidence from different sources that support the claim, does not explain how each source supports the claim, and cites the source for each example; OR

is evidence based, provides 2 pieces of evidence from a single source that supports the claim, explains how that example supports the claim, and cites the source; OR

is evidence based, provides 1 piece of evidence from a single source that supports the claim, explains how that example supports the claim, and cites the source; OR

is evidence based, provides 2 pieces of evidence from different sources that support the claim, explains how each example supports the claim, and does NOT cite sources.

An example of a response worth 1 point is: An exemplar example of a response worth 2 points is: The cell phone was not as user friendly as it is now. When it was first invented, it was hard for people to get a hold of and it was hard for people to use. For example, Source #2 says that the first cell phone cost almost $4,000. This is important because this means that only the richest people could afford cell phones. This also means that most people couldn't even have access to a cell phone at first.

A response worth 0 points is: incorrect, irrelevant, insufficient, and blank. An example of a response worth 0 points is: Cell phones were not user friendly at first. They were only made for cars and cost over $4,000. **(3.W.1.b, 3.RI.9)**

3. **See detailed explanation**.

Apple introduced the first iPhone in 2007: Source #1

Dr. Martin Cooper and his wife invented the Jitterbug: Source #2

Today's phones have access to the internet, many apps, and touch screens: Source #1, Source #2

Dr. Martin Cooper made the first phone call on a handheld device in 1973: Source #1, Source #2

1 point: all 3 cells completed correctly

0 points: Fewer than 3 cells completed correctly or blank **(3.W.8, 3.RI.9)**

4. **See detailed explanation.** When scoring a student's informational article, you should examine the following components: Organzation/Purpose; Development/Elaboration; and Writing Conventions.

This includes that the student: shows a clear understanding of what information was required, and who the audience is; writes about one clear topic; uses plenty of details to support topic; writing is well organized; uses transitions well, and the order of information makes good sense; demonstrates an excellent use of language and sentence structure; tone is clear, is easy to read and understand; uses a variety of sentence structures is easy to read and understand; and has few errors in grammar, usage, spelling, and punctuation. The errors that are there do not make the writing unclear.

**(3.W.3.a, 3.W.3.b, 3.W.3.c, 3.W.3.d, 3.L.3.a, 3.L.6, 3.L.1, 3.L.2, 3.W.8)**

# BONUS
## FULL-LENGTH
## PRACTICE TEST

### GO TO THE FOLLOWING URL ADDRESS
### TO ACCESS YOUR BONUS PRACTICE TEST.

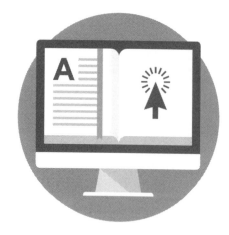

## https://originstutoring.lpages.co/sbac-ela-grade-3/

Thank you for selecting this book.

We would be thrilled if you left us a review on

the website where you bought this book!

Made in the USA
Las Vegas, NV
26 January 2023

66294380R00074